God's Gift – We are Conceived Heirs of God
ISBN 978-0-692-15856-2

Copyright © 2018 by Paul E. LaForge

LaForge Books
An imprint of Paul E. LaForge
8170 W. Valley View Drive
Skiatook, OK 74070

Printed in the United States of America.

Unless indicated otherwise, all Scripture quotations are taken from *NKJV*.

Scriptures marked *NKJV* are taken from the *NEW KING JAMES VERSION (NKJV):* Scripture taken from the *NEW KING JAMES VERSION®*. Copyright© 1982 by Thomas Nelson, Inc. Used by Gratus Use permission.

Scriptures marked *KJV* are taken from the *KING JAMES VERSION (KJV): KING JAMES VERSION*, public domain.

Scriptures marked *NSECB* are abbreviated definitions. They are taken from *NEW STRONG'S EXHAUSTIVE CONCORDANCE OF THE BIBLE* by James Strong LL.D. S.T.D. Copyright© 1984 by Thomas Nelson. Used by permission of Thomas Nelson. www.thomasnelson.com.

The Appendix A List of Denominations is a summary listing taken from *Handbook of Denominations in the United States, 11th Edition*. Copyright© 1985, 1990, 1995, 2001 by Abingdon Press. Used by permission of Abingdon Press.

The Appendix B definitions are derived and summarized from *Sparkling Gems from the Greek (Volume I)*. Copyright© 2003 by Rick Renner. Used by permission of Rick Renner.

1

Acknowledgments

To Alison, my wife and partner – her heart for Jesus is paramount. Through countless discussions and manuscript drafts, together we came to a much deeper discernment and appreciation of the awe-inspiring reality of God's gift.

To Alec Bates for his spiritual and structural critiques. His insightful commentaries and technical suggestions were influential in writing a much more understandable and flowing composition.

To Tiffany Zamora for her numerous *"I just don't get it"* quandaries and questions. Her zeal for understanding the truth was instrumental in forcing multiple re-writes until arriving at those *"now I get it"* moments.

To Gary McIntosh for his spiritual and pastoral guidance. Our many discussions were influential in portraying the true meanings of God's Word.

—— ♦ ——

Are you saved?

Are you born again?

When were you saved?

When were you born again?

What part did you perform?

What part did Jesus perform?

What does confess really mean?

Do you wonder about eternal life?

Can you reject your inheritance?

Can you lose your inheritance?

Are you in the book of life?

What is blaspheming?

What is overcoming?

Do you even care?

—— ♦ ——

What does God's Word say?

—— ♦ ——

———— ♦ ————

It was during a typical Sunday class when people were discoursing about that "aha moment" when they were saved – usually at a church camp or something similar. I mentioned that I didn't recall any particular "aha moment" and that my believing and getting to know Jesus was more of a gradual growing process. A voice in the back of the room quickly countered that if I did not have an "aha moment" then I wasn't saved – my inner feelings were that if there ever was a self-righteous leader it would likely be him. Sadly, at the same time my inner feelings were also questioning my salvation status.

I went to a few more Sunday classes, but kept my thoughts to myself – no reason to ruffle the comfort zone of status quo. I eventually departed with a mission to look directly into God's thoughts on the issue – into God's owner's manual. The Bible appeared to be the best source for learning. So began the journey.

What does God's Word say?

I pursued my Bible research in much the same way I have pursued secular work research – sorting fact from opinion – sorting translation from interpretation. I definitely did not start with the idea of authoring a written manuscript. My goal was to let the Holy Spirit, not man, guide me in my learning. My plan was to use my word processor as a good way to take a few notes – but the notes just kept growing. Alison, my wife, quickly became my accountability partner and critic – her heart for Jesus is paramount. Together we learned that there exists conflicting and dividing denominational theology, such that not every theology can be right. WOW – what a journey – what a clear revelation. This manuscript is the unfolding result of our growth and enlightenment by the Holy Spirit.

———— ♦ ————

INTRODUCTION

PART I ~ I Am A Born Again Heir of God

PART II ~ Preserving My Birthright Inheritance

PART III ~ Appendices

Introduction

A Kingdom

Jesus refers to the *kingdom* of heaven and the *kingdom* of God.

When referring to the *kingdom*, God's Word does NOT make a single reference or allusion to a democracy of God, or a democratic republic of God, or a convention of God, or a social movement of God, or etc., or etc. …

The simple fact is that Jesus always uses the term *kingdom*. In a *kingdom*, only the King has ruling authority – no one else has any authority to change, modernize, upgrade, downgrade, loosen or tighten the King's word. No denomination, no pastor, no dreamer, no liberal, no conservative, no politician, no judge, no parent, no teacher, no PhD, no social movement, no etc., no etc. has any authority whatsoever to change the King's edict. Until the King himself changes an edict, nothing changes.

In the United States there are approximately 200 diverse denominational organizations (Appendix A) that label themselves a church – in God's kingdom there is only one. Although the founders' underlying motives were well-intentioned, the unfortunate reality is that most of these churches were birthed into churches of rejection – i.e., birthed by rejecting *some* of the teachings and disciples of their predecessor affiliation while trying to retain some core underlying theology. The current teachings of the diverse denominational theologies are now all over the map, with many sprouting religious doctrines in direct conflict with each other. In a departure from denomination based theology, the non-denominational movement is striving for a theology based on God's Word. It is a simple truth that the multitude of conflicting doctrines cannot all be right.

For example, try asking someone what happens to a child who dies at the age of 4. Get ready for a trip around the globe. Some say baptize them at birth. Some say God takes care of children. Some hope God takes care of children. Some say children have imputed sin, but are innocent until they know right from wrong. Some say the Word does not directly enlighten us on this issue. Some say they simply don't know. So where do we turn to get the truth?

The answer is simple. Our manuscript looks earnestly into *What God Says* about the concepts and issues – *it is God's opinion that matters*. Since interpretive opinion often skews the translation from Hebrew to Greek and Greek to English, we searched the original Hebrew and Greek meaning – i.e., back to the source. We do foresee that our manuscript will be perceived by some as so what, by some as a controversial misguided challenge, by others as a Bible based enlightenment.

In a Nutshell

In our search, we learned that man, not God, has made the Word complicated. *God's* theology and *religion's* theology are often *different* with religion's assorted intermingling of grace, works, confession, repentance, conviction, born again, kingdom of heaven, heaven, salvation and eternal life. It is no wonder that I was in a spiritual quandary and confused about salvation.

I was so sure that Santa, Easter Bunnies and Goblins were real creatures.

I was so sure that I was hell bound without a priest forgiving my mortal sins…
…but no one could seem to clearly define mortal verses venial sins.

I was so sure that Catholic nuns never clashed…
…I came to realize that nuns are human.

I was so sure that Catholic priests were above reproach…
…I came to realize that priests are human.

I was so sure that I wanted to go into the seminary out of the 8th grade…
…I came to realize that lifetime celibacy did not appeal to me.

I was so sure that Catholics get a better heaven seat than Protestants…
…I came to realize that Catholics are not holier than Protestants.

I was so sure that Protestant ministers were above reproach…
…I came to realize that ministers are human.

I was so sure that I was born a lost soul and had to perform works to be saved…
…I came to realize that denominational dictums often contain erroneous dogmas.

Religion usually teaches that Jesus died for our sins; but *unofficially* communicates works, repeated alter calls, shame and guilt, maybe not good enough, etc., etc. with the *underlying* message being:
(i) everyone is born *lost/condemned*, and
(ii) although Jesus' last breath declared it is finished, it doesn't really mean finished since human effort (cloaked works) is required to attain a *forgiven / born again / saved* status.

God's Word teaches a simple *heir of God* relationship where:
(i) everyone is conceived in the womb as a *born again* heir *of God* with all the benefits of family eternal life inheritance, and
(ii) it is not about doing all the right stuff to become a part of God's family, but rather it is about *overcoming* and *submitting to* (*not blaspheming*) the guidance of the Holy Spirit and *preserving* (*not rejecting*) our birthright eternal life inheritance.

Adam and Eve were created *inside* God's family, walking and talking with God. Satan convinced them to believe that God was holding out on them.

I too must choose who and what to believe.

Religion usually teaches I am born *outside* (*separated from God*) and that I must repent via cloaked works while hoping *to get inside* with the family of Jesus.

God's Word teaches I am born *inside (in God's family)* with the Holy Spirit living in me and shepherding me to overcome the worldly temptation to follow my flesh *to the outside*.

I *begin* my journey as a *born again* heir of God. Then, as I reach the age of *understanding*, John 3:16 comes into play and I must mature by refocusing my belief, faith and trust from my earthly parents to a full belief, faith and trust in Jesus (God has no grandchildren).

Proverbs 22:6 teaches, *"Train a child in the way he should go, and when he is old he will not turn from it."*

1Peter 4:9 teaches *"Be hospitable to one another without grumbling. As each one has received a gift, minister it to one another, as good stewards of the manifold grace of God."*

As growing children and maturing adults, wherein each of us is *born inside God's family*:
• we help each other *preserve* our inheritance of eternal life with Jesus,
• we help each other *overcome* our own EGO (**E**dge **G**od **O**ut) spirit,
• we help each other *elude* blaspheming the Holy Spirit that resides in each of us (*the unforgiveable sin*) – i.e., *elude* becoming a house divided, and
• we help each other *avoid* the EGO trap of *rejecting* our born again birthright inheritance.

God entrusts every single one of us with grace-given special gifts to help one another – God is depending upon each of us *as members of His family* to be faithful in helping each other overcome worldly temptations. We must *surrender* to our Father and help each other preserve our *birthright* salvation status.

To comprehend my child of God *forgiven / born again / saved* status in the covenant between God and Jesus, I must *acknowledge* the reality of a Time Paradox – I did not say *fully understand*. In the Old Testament, God refers to himself as *"I am"*. In the New Testament, Jesus refers to himself as *"I am"* – NOT ***I was*** – NOT ***I will be***.

A Time Paradox is manifested when we read in Revelations about *"the Lamb slain from the foundation [creation] of the world"* [Rev 13:8]. But how could this be since this is the same Lamb [Jesus] that was born only a couple of thousand years ago? The simple fact is that I cannot wrap my *finite* brain around this Time Paradox thing – I can acknowledge only that it exists. Once I concede to the reality of the Time Paradox, I open the door for discerning God's Word and the pure grace in God's plan for my salvation. In this manifested Time Paradox, God is allowing my brief *finite flesh* existence [James 4:14] to freely choose my *infinite spiritual* existence – to *stay with* or to *leave* my birthright family.

The Prodigal Son
Luke 15:11

Jesus' prodigal son parable is a compelling summary of God's pure grace plan and my free will to choose. Jesus' parable introduces us to two sons who were born into a family – each with a birthright inheritance – with neither son having any say in their birthright status. As the one son matured and reached the age of *understanding*, he made a free will choice to exploit his *grace gift worldly inheritance* and turn away from his family for some time, until eventually repenting and returning to his family. The now insightful and repenting prodigal son is revealed in *"But when he came to himself, he said... I will arise and go to my father, and will say to him, Father, I have sinned against heaven and before you."* The heart of the yearning and watching father is revealed in *"But when he was still a great way off, his father saw him and had compassion, and ran and fell on his neck and kissed him."* The other son complained *"Lo, these many years I have been serving you; I never transgressed your commandment at any time; and yet you never gave me a young goat, that I might make merry with my friends. But as soon as this son of yours came, who has devoured your livelihood with harlots, you killed the fatted calf for him."* The elated father then explained to the other son *"Son, you are always with me, and all that I have is yours. It was right that we should make merry and be glad, for your brother was dead and is alive again, and was lost and is found."*

- The phrase *"When he came to himself"* illustrates the maturing prodigal son now understanding, realizing, and admitting that it was *his* free will choice to reject life with his family.
- The phrase *"I will arise and go to my father, and will say to him, Father, I have sinned against heaven and before you."* illustrates the prodigal son repenting and agreeing (confessing) that it had been *his* rash free will choice to sin against heaven and his father, but is now *surrendering* to his father.
- The phrase *"But when he was still a great way off, his father saw him and had compassion"* illustrates a loving father yearning and watching for the return of his child.
- The phrase *"and ran and fell on his neck and kissed him"* portrays an excited and forgiving father running to accept, protect and affirm his love for his returning child. In Jewish tradition, a son who had lost his wealth among the gentiles and so dishonored his father would be cut off and rejected by the community. The father was protecting his son with his best robe, ring and sandals – the father's righteousness. Despite what he had previously done, the

son had returned – the father was displaying to the entire community that his son was assuredly welcome back as his child.

- The phrase *"Lo, these many years I have been serving you"* depicts resentful Pharisees and Christians who profess a *faith-based* theology, but in reality live a *works-based* theology.
- The phrase *"Son, you are always with me, and all that I have is yours"* illustrates the story of the all too typical Christian who simply will not accept and comprehend that eternal life is a birthright inheritance.
- The phrases *"alive again"* and *"was lost"* depict (i) being *conceived born alive*, (ii) then *choosing to be lost* with the world, and (iii) finally repenting to *being alive again* in Jesus.

The message – Both sons began life born into the family with the *grace gift* of a birthright inheritance – the sons had no say in the matter. Then, one son made a rash free will choice to reject his family until finally coming to his sense, repenting and returning to his family. The father welcomed this prodigal son back with open arms. The other son, a churched *works-based* Christian simply did not believe and accept the reality of the birthright *grace gift* of eternal life with Jesus.

At the Cross

While nailed to the cross and still alive, Jesus' final words reveal insightful perspectives – some of these perspectives are rarely explored from the pulpits. We see Jesus allowing free will choice to determine eternal destiny – i.e., unilaterally interceding for the sins against a man, but not interceding for blasphemy against the Spirit. We see a time paradox of *finite* vs *infinite*.

- While addressing the Pharisees, Jesus said to them, *"Therefore I say to you, every sin and blasphemy will be forgiven men, but the blasphemy against the Spirit will not be forgiven men."* ^Matt 12:31^ Later at the cross, for the loyal soldiers casting lots for his clothing, Jesus interceded saying *"Father, forgive them for they do not know what they do."* ^Luke 23:34^ These soldiers were submitting to Roman authority, albeit ignorantly, rather than being their own show – they were not a subversion threat to authority and not creating a *house divided against itself*. The soldier's actions were against the Son of man – they were not blaspheming the *Spirit* – Jesus interceded for them.
- For the criminal on His one side, whose *heart and spirit* prayed and submitted to Jesus, Jesus assured him *"... today you will be with Me in Paradise."* ^Luke 23:43^ The first fundamental principal is Jesus' intercession – a fairly common teaching. A second fundamental principal is revealed in the *"I am"* Jesus' reference to *"today"* – not on the third day – not at the resurrection – rather, *"today"* Jesus and the criminal celebrate the *infinite* eternal realm as manifested *finite* flesh expires. I can only acknowledge (I did not say comprehend) the existence of a *finite* vs *infinite* time paradox.
- For the criminal to His other side, who boastfully blasphemed the *Spirit* in him and exposed his own *house divided heart and spirit*, Jesus made no intercession of any kind. Jesus simply allowed him to remain the prodigal son who chose to leave and not return.

10

Is this relevant and applicable to me/us today? An emphatic Yes! Hebrews tells us *"Jesus Christ is the same yesterday, today, and forever."* [Heb 13:8] Jesus does not change the rules. Jesus is looking at my heart and spirit. The answer is really quite simple. Jesus desires an *eternal relationship* with His family. *"...Behold, the tabernacle of God is with men, and He will dwell with them, and they shall be His people. God Himself will be with them and be their God* [Rev 21:3]

What God's Word Says

Part I, I Am A Born Again Heir of God. We study the Time Paradox of a co-existent *finite* and *infinite*, God's grace gift in the New Covenant, a Book of Life and how each of us begins *finite* life *born again* with Jesus as an *heir of God* – I have no say in my being conceived a *born again* heir in God's family.

Part II, Preserving My Birthright Inheritance. We study free will choice – and *choose we must* – laissez-fair indifference simply won't cut it. As I reach the age of *understanding and hear the Word*, I must *receive* the kingdom of God like a little child – put my full faith and trust in Jesus. We study the worldly spirit's enticement to blaspheme the Holy Spirit and create in me a *spiritual house divided*. We learned that blasphemy against the Holy Spirit is not what is generally perceived. Good, as measured by the world, just might be blasphemy – then again maybe not. Bad, as measure by a church, just might not be blasphemy – then again maybe yes. In Part II and in Appendix B we explore the subtle deception in blasphemous acts against the Holy Spirit. It is my *life vs death choice – blasphemy against the Holy Spirit residing inside me is the unforgiveable sin* – I must refute and *overcome* these worldly deception and enticements.

———— ♦ ————

Most of humanity exists in a constant struggle to bridge the infinite abyss between imperfect mankind and a perfect God – between earth and paradise – between finite death and eternal life. By faith I *surrender* to God as my loving Father. By faith I *accept* God's perfect plan. If I follow a journey that tries to add to what God has already done, I destroy my capacity to benefit from it.

While discussing God's plan with a family pastor, he asked a very relevant question. "But what would an *altar call invitation* look like? The answer – preach as a fellow birthright *"heir of God through Christ"* [Gal 4:7] with an *altar call invitation* (i) to absorb that each of us is conceived an heir of God – cleansed by Jesus' sacrifice – born again by Jesus' resurrection, (ii) to connect with each other as family in Jesus, (iii) to accept Jesus as my Lord, and (iv) to both call upon and support each other in overcoming the prodigal temptations of the world.

"Our greatest fear as individuals and as a church should not be of failure, but of succeeding at things in life that don't really matter." [Francis Chan] Rather than become a *"did it my way"* spiritual house divided, I choose to bask in the glorious gift from God and follow the voice of the Holy Spirit that is residing inside me.

PART I

I Am A Born Again Heir of God

Chapter 1
The TIME PARADOX

Reality is a Time Paradox with co-existing infinite spirit *and* finite flesh.
By acknowledging this dichotomy, God's Word suddenly came into focus.
Seemingly contradictory verses suddenly became harmonic.

I AM

My first trek into this Time Paradox sprouted to life with the words *"I am"*. The concept of *I am* and "eternal life" is beyond my mortal ability to fully comprehend. Eternity has no past and no future – it seems to be a perpetual state of now. A thousand years ago is today for *I am* – A thousand years from now is today for *I am*. In the Old Testament, God identified himself to Moses as *I am*. In the New Testament, Jesus boldly affirmed that He is the great *I am* of the Old Testament. So how could this be if Jesus was born only 33 years earlier? The following *I am* scriptures spawned in me a new awareness of the *infinite* for both God and Jesus.

NKJV Scripture	NSECB Definitions
LaForge Commentary. In the following biblical citations, words with the superscript[9999] are not found in the original Greek manuscripts, but rather are words that have been added by modern day translators. In the following **I am** scriptures, many translators change the biblical message by adding the word He[9999]. The addition of He[9999] totally changes the context. Similarly, in John 6:20, **I am** is improperly translated **It is I**. When properly translated as **I am**, the words of God and Jesus inexplicably proclaim *infinite existence* – on the other hand, **I am** He[9999] and **It is I** merely convey an *identity acknowledgment*.	
Exo 03:14. And God said to Moses, "I AM[1961] WHO I AM[1961]." And He said, "Thus you shall say to the children of Israel, 'I AM[1961] has sent me to you.'"	[1961]**I AM.** a primitive root [compare 1933]; to exist, i.e. be or become, come to pass (always emphatic, and not a mere copula or auxiliary).
John 4:25-26. The woman said to Him, "I know that Messiah is coming" (who is called Christ). "When He comes, He will tell us all things." Jesus said to her, "I[1473] who speak to you am[1510] He[9999]." *Greek interlinear reads:* "I[1473] am[1510] he[9999] that speak unto thee"	[1473]**I.** a primary pronoun of the first person I (only expressed when emphatic).
John 6:19-20. So when they had rowed about three or four miles, they saw Jesus walking on the sea and drawing near the boat; and they were afraid. But He said to them, "It is[1510] I[1473]; do not be afraid." *Greek interlinear reads:* "I[1473] am[1510]; not be afraid."	
John 8:58. Jesus said to them, "Most assuredly, I say to you, before Abraham was, I[1473] am[1510]."	[1510]**am.** the first person singular present indicative; a prolonged form of a primary and defective verb; I exist (used only when emphatic).
John 13:19-21. "Now I tell you before it comes, that when it does come to pass, you may believe that I[1473] am[1510] He[9999]. Most assuredly, I say to you, he who receives whomever I send receives Me; and he who receives Me receives Him who sent Me." When Jesus had said these things, He was troubled in spirit, and testified and said, "Most assuredly, I say to you, one of you will betray Me."	[4686]**detachment.** A Roman Cohort or military guard, consisting of 480
John 18:3-9. Then Judas, having received a detachment[4686] of troops[9999], and officers from the chief priests and Pharisees, came there with lanterns, torches,	

and weapons. Jesus therefore, knowing all things that would come upon Him, went forward and said to them, "Whom are you seeking?" They answered Him, "Jesus of Nazareth." Jesus said to them, "I[1473] am[1510] He[9999]." And Judas, who betrayed Him, also stood with them. Now when He said to them, "I[1473] am[1510] He[9999]," they drew back and fell[4098] to the ground[5476]. Then He asked them again, "Whom are you seeking?" And they said, "Jesus of Nazareth." Jesus answered, "I have told you that I[1473] am[1510] He[9999]. Therefore, if you seek Me, let these go their way," that the saying might be fulfilled which He spoke, "Of those whom You gave Me I have lost none."

[4098]**fell.** To fall prostrate.
[5476]**ground.** Earthward, i.e. prostrate.
[9999]. Inserted word; not in the original Greek.

The above scriptures condense into simple *"I am"* proclamation statements.

- When Moses asked God his name, God said to Moses *"I AM [hayah] WHO I AM [hayah] ... Thus you shall say to the children of Israel, 'I AM [hayah] has sent me to you.'" Exo 3:14*.

- When Jesus was speaking to the Samaritan lady at the well, He identified himself as *"I am [egoo eimi]" John 4:25*.

- When Jesus calmed His apostles' fears in the stormy Sea of Galilee, He identified himself as *"I am [egoo eimi]; not be afraid" John 6:20*.

- When Jesus was addressing the Jews, He identified himself as *"Before Abraham was, I am [egoo eimi]" John 8:58*.

- At the last supper, Jesus identified himself to the apostles as *"I am [egoo eimi]" John 13:19*.

- When the Roman soldiers were preparing to arrest Jesus, He identified himself twice as *"I am [egoo eimi]" John 18:5 & 18:8*.

Both the Hebrew *[hayah]* and the Greek *[ego eimi]* mean *to exist* or *I exist* – these two words do *not* convey any concept of *past* or *future*.

———— ◆ ————

As an interesting side note, I also found it quite revealing that Jesus speaking *I am [egoo eimi]* to the Roman soldiers was so God powerful that it knocked the 480± soldiers prostrate to the ground. *John 18:5-6* Jesus was not taken by force; Jesus *surrendered* voluntarily because it was his Father's will. A central theme of Jesus' *(I am)* manifestation on earth was *"submission and obedience"* to the will of His Father *(I am)*.

———— ◆ ————

Much of God's Word speaks to us in *finite* parables to help us arrive at some measure of understanding *infinite* eternal life. In my flesh nature I exist in terms of *past-present-future*, whereas infinite exists only in terms of the *present*. *Finite flesh* exists within man's bounds and limits during this current age – *flesh* bounds and limits do not exist in the *spirit* eternal life realm – eternal life simply "exists". There is a difference between *finite flesh* and *infinite spirit*.

- **My Flesh life is *finite* – mortal.**
- **My Spirit life is *infinite* – eternal.**
- **God's Word and parables speak to both the *finite* and the *infinite*.**

Jesus and Creation

In my former days, John 1:1-3 made absolutely no sense to me – poetically quaint, but gibberish – that is until I recognized the manifested co-existence of *infinite spirit* and my *finite flesh*. When I accept this, I understand that Jesus' human birth in Bethlehem was not His beginning but merely *His finite manifestation to man* – a brief appearance within His *infinite* existence. The following scriptures reveal the infinite Jesus as the creator of *all* and the heir of *all*.

NKJV Scripture	NSECB Definitions
John 1:1-3, 14. In the beginning[0746] was the Word, and the Word was with God, and the Word was God. He was in the beginning[0746] with God. **All things were made[1096] through Him**, and without Him nothing was made[1096] that was made[1096]... **John 1:14. And the Word became[1096] flesh[4561] and dwelt among us,** and we beheld His glory, the glory as of the only begotten of the Father, full of grace and truth.	[0165]**worlds.** properly, an age; by extension, perpetuity (also past); by implication, the world. [0746]**beginning.** a commencement, or chief (in various applications of order, time, place, or rank). [1096]**made, became.** a prolongation and middle voice form of a primary verb; to cause to be, ("gen"- erate), i.e. (reflexively) to become (come into being), used with great latitude. [2602]**foundation.** a deposition, i.e. founding; figuratively, conception.
Col 1:15-16. He is the image of the invisible God, the firstborn over all creation. For by Him all things were created[2936] that are in heaven and that are on earth, visible and invisible, whether thrones or dominions or principalities or powers. **All things were created[2936] through Him and for Him.**	[2889]**world.** orderly arrangement, i.e. decoration; by implication, the world (in a wide or narrow sense, including its inhabitants, literally or figuratively [morally]). [2936]**created.** probably akin to 2932 (through the idea of proprietor-ship of the manufacturer); to fabricate, i.e. found (form originally).
Heb 1:1-2. God, who at various times and in various ways spoke in time past to the fathers by the prophets, has in these last days spoken to us by His Son, **whom He has appointed heir of all things,** through whom also He made the worlds[0165];	[4253]**before.** a primary preposition; "fore", i.e. in front of, prior (figuratively, superior) to. [4561]**flesh.** flesh (as stripped of the skin), i.e. (strictly) the meat of an animal (as food), or (by extension) the body (as opposed to the soul [or spirit], or as the symbol of what is external, or as the means of kindred), or (by implication) human nature (with its frailties [physically or morally] and passions), or (specifically) a human being (as such).
1 Peter 1:20. He *[Jesus]* indeed was foreordained before[4253] the foundation[2602] of the world[2889], but was manifest in these last times for you...	

The Bible gives us a picture of creation. The reality of *"I am [egoo eimi]"* unfolds before us where the *infinite* Jesus as the manifested Word both *is God* and *with God* at the beginning of the *finite world* creation. *John 1:1* The above scriptures condense into simple creation statements.

- **Jesus was chosen by God before the creation of the finite world.** *1Pet 1:20*
- **Jesus was manifested to us in these last days for our sake.** *1Pet 1:20*
- *All* **of creation was made through Jesus** *John 1:3*
- *All* **of creation was made by and for Jesus** *Col 1:16*
- **God appointed Jesus the heir of** *all* **creation –** *nothing is excluded.* *Heb 1:2*
- **The** *infinite* **Word Jesus became flesh and entered into His creation's** *finite* **world timeline to dwell among His creation.** *John 1:14*

Jesus and Victory

I just *knew* that the slain Jesus didn't exist until around 2,000 years ago...
...I had to remap my thinking.

When I look at scripture regarding the slain Jesus, I see a time paradox – I see two paradigms of *infinite* and *finite* continuing to emerge. I see Jesus at the beginning of creation, but with another twist – I see the Jesus that was slain from the creation of the world, and also the Jesus that was slain around 2,000 years ago. The following scriptures proclaim Jesus overcoming the world even before His death on the cross – as the Lamb slain from the foundation [creation] of the world.

NKJV Scripture	NSECB Definitions
Luke 10:18-20. And He said to them, "I saw[2334] **Satan fall like lightning from heaven.** Behold, I give you the authority to trample on serpents and scorpions, and over all the power of the enemy, and nothing shall by any means hurt you. Nevertheless do not rejoice in this, that the spirits are subject to you, but rather **rejoice because your names are written in heaven.**"	[2334]**saw.** to be a spectator of, i.e. discern, (literally, figuratively [experience] or intensively [acknowledge]).
John 16:33. These things I have spoken to you, that in Me you may have peace. In the world you will have tribulation[2347]; but be of good cheer, **I have overcome[3528] the world[2889].**" *LaForge Commentary.* Jesus' death and resurrection had not yet been manifested in the finite realm.	[2347]**tribulation.** pressure (literally or figuratively). [2512]**purged.** a washing off, i.e. (cer.) ablution, (morally) expiation. [2602]**foundation.** a deposition, i.e. founding; figuratively, conception.
John 17:1-5. Jesus spoke these words, lifted up His eyes to heaven, and said: "Father, the hour has come. Glorify Your Son, that Your Son also may glorify You, as **You [Father] have given Him [Jesus] authority over all flesh, that He [Jesus] should give eternal life to as many as You [Father] have given Him [Jesus].** And this is eternal life, that they may know You, the only true God, and Jesus Christ whom You have sent. I have glorified You on the earth. **I have finished the work which You have given Me to do.** And now, **O Father, glorify Me together with Yourself, with the glory which I had with You before the world[2889] was.**"	[2889]**world.** orderly arrangement, i.e. decoration; by implication, the world (in a wide or narrow sense, including its inhabitants, literally or figuratively [morally]). [3528]**have overcome.** to subdue (literally or figuratively). [4969]**slain.** a primary verb; to butcher (especially an animal for food or in sacrifice) or (generally) to slaughter, or (specifically) to maim (violently).
Heb 1:3. who being the brightness of His glory and the express image of His person, and upholding all things by the word of His power, **when He had by Himself purged[2512] our sins, sat down at the right hand of the Majesty on high,**	
Rev 13:8. All who dwell on the earth will worship him, whose names have not been written in **the Book of Life of the Lamb slain[4969] from the foundation[2602] of the world[2889].**	

While Jesus was on earth conversing with his apostles, He revealed that He *"saw Satan fall like lightning from heaven"*. ^{Luke 10:18} He instructed his apostles to *"rejoice because your names are written in heaven"*. ^{Luke 10:20} He also revealed that He had already *"overcome the world"* ^{John 16:33} even though the *finite manifestation* of His death and resurrection had not yet occurred.

In the garden of Gethsemane, Jesus is praying to the Father regarding His impending death and resurrection mission – regarding the Father giving Jesus' *"authority over all flesh, that He should give eternal life to as many as You [Father] have given Him [Jesus]"* ^{John 17:2}. Jesus' prayers focus on the *Father and Jesus* giving – the focus is on *Jesus* performing – the covenant between God and Jesus – nowhere is there any mention of *man* performing. Jesus then proclaims *"I have finished the work which You have given Me to do"* ^{John 17:4} and concludes with *"O Father, glorify Me together with Yourself, with the glory which I had with You before the world was."* ^{John 17:5} Jesus' victory occurred with *His total surrender to the Father* – the cross was the finite manifestation of *His surrender*. In all of this, Jesus is speaking about His *infinite* mission that preceded His *finite* manifestation – the mystery of the Time Paradox.

———— ♦ ————

In the preceding scriptures, I learned about Jesus (i) overcoming the world, (ii) purging my sins and (iii) writing my name in the Book of Life of the Lamb. In the following scriptures, I learn of my *being born sealed/marked by the Holy Spirit* of God for the day Jesus redeems me as His bought and paid-for possession.

NKJV Scripture	NSECB Definitions
Eph 4:30. And do not grieve³⁰⁷⁶ the **Holy Spirit of God, by whom you were sealed⁴⁹⁷² for the day of redemption⁰⁶²⁹**.	⁰⁰⁵⁹**you were bought.** properly, to go to market, i.e. (by implication) to purchase; specially, to redeem. ⁰⁶²⁹**redemption.** (the act) ransom in full, i.e. (figuratively) riddance, or (specially) Christian salvation.
1Peter 1:18-20. knowing that **you were not redeemed³⁰⁸⁴ with corruptible things**, like silver or gold, from your aimless conduct received by tradition from your fathers, **but with the precious blood of Christ, as of a lamb without blemish and without spot.** He indeed was **foreordained before the foundation²⁶⁰² of the world²⁸⁸⁹, but was manifest in these last times for you**	²⁶⁰²**foundation.** a deposition, i.e. founding; figuratively, conception. ²⁸⁸⁹**world.** orderly arrangement, i.e. decoration; by implication, the world (in a wide or narrow sense, including its inhabitants, literally or figuratively [morally]). ³⁰⁷⁶**grieve.** to distress; reflexively or passively, to be sad. ³⁰⁸⁴**you were not redeemed.** to ransom (literally or figuratively). ⁴⁹⁷²**you were sealed.** to stamp (with a signet or private mark) for security or preservation (literally or figuratively); by implication, to keep secret, to attest.
1Cor 6:19-20. Or do you not know that **your body is the temple of the Holy Spirit who is in you,** whom you have from God, and **you are not your own? For you were bought⁰⁰⁵⁹ at a price⁵⁰⁹²**; therefore glorify God in your body and in your spirit, which are God's.	⁵⁰⁹²**price.** a value, i.e. money paid, or (concretely and collectively) valuables; by analogy, esteem (especially of the highest degree), or the dignity itself.

In simple terms, I am sealed by the Holy Spirit for a day of redemption through the precious blood of Christ as the manifested lamb who was foreordained before the creation of the world – I am the temple of the Holy Spirit – I am not my own, but rather, I belong to Jesus.

———— ♦ ————

In summary, for me, it was not too difficult to reason that Jesus was *chosen* before the foundation [creation] of the world *1Pet 1:20* – reasonable *finite* logic. However, the ultimate paradox of Jesus' *infinite* victory comes from John's "Book of Revelation" with the words "*the Lamb slain from the foundation [creation] of the world.*" *Rev 13:8* I cannot wrap my *finite* brain around the Time Paradox – I can only accept the paradox.

- **The *infinite* Jesus' death and resurrection is before *finite* creation.** *Rev 13:8*
- **Jesus' victory over Satan is *before* Jesus' *manifested finite* death.** *John 16:33*
- **I am born sealed/marked as Jesus' bought and paid-for possession.** *1Cor 6:19*
- **With the *finite* Jesus having victoriously purged my sins and having completed His manifestation on earth, the *infinite* Jesus sat down at the right hand of the *infinite* Majesty in heaven.** *Heb 1:3*

The Reality of Eternity

I had read the Bible a few times and had heard all about eternal life, damnation, hell and eternal death. Now something fundamental is maturing within me – the deepening awareness of *finite flesh* verses *infinite spirit*.

finite is temporary reality – *infinite* is true reality

The reality of eternity is all too often minimized and/or not even discussed. At this juncture I must come face-to-face with the reality of my eternal destiny – the reality that infinite is a very, very, very, very long existence. The following scriptures reveal the co-existence of my vanishing temporary *flesh* reality and my eternal *spirit* reality.

NKJV Scripture	NSECB Definitions
Matt 26:40-41. Then He came to the disciples and found them sleeping, and said to Peter, "What! Could you not watch with Me one hour? **Watch and pray, lest you enter into temptation. The spirit[4151] indeed is willing[4289], but the flesh[4561] is weak[0772].**"	[0772]**weak.** strengthless (in various applications, literal, figurative and moral). [0822]**vapor.** mist. [0853]**vanishes.** to render unapparent, i.e. (actively) consume (becloud), or (passively) disappear (be destroyed). [4151]**spirit.** a current of air, i.e. breath (blast) or a breeze; by analogy or figuratively, a spirit, i.e. (human) the rational soul, (by implication) vital principle, mental disposition, etc., or (superhuman) an angel, demon, or (divine) God, Christ's spirit, the Holy Spirit.
James 4:13-16. Come now, you who say, "Today or tomorrow we will go to such and such a city, spend a year there, buy and sell, and make a profit"; **whereas you do not know what will happen tomorrow. For what is your life? It is even a vapor[0822] that appears[5316] for a little time and then**	[4289]**willing.** forward in spirit, i.e. predisposed; neuter (as noun) alacrity. [4561]**flesh.** flesh (as stripped of the skin), i.e. (strictly) the meat of an animal (as food), or (by extension) the body (as opposed to the soul [or spirit], or as the symbol of what is external, or as the means of kindred), or (by implication) human nature (with its

vanishes[0853] **away.** Instead you ought to say, "If the Lord wills, we shall live and do this or that." But now you boast in your arrogance. All such boasting is evil.

frailties [physically or morally] and passions), or (specifically) a human being (as such).
[5316]**appears.** to lighten (shine), i.e. show (transitive or intransitive, literal or figurative).

Jesus makes a clear distinction between *spirit* verse *flesh* – the disciple's *spirits* wanted to do the right thing, but their *flesh* took control. *Matt 26:41* James, in referring to the *flesh*, speaks of *"a vapor that appears for a little while and then vanishes." James 4:14* Both Jesus and James are quite clear that *spirit* verses *flesh* is more than some academic exercise. The impulses of my temporary *flesh* are in a constant battle for control over the eternal destiny of my permanent *spirit*.

I must choose wisely.
Eternity is a very, very, very, very long existence.

All of my desires, emotions and feeling reside in my *spirit* that lives on for eternity. My *flesh* is simply a brief cocoon (a mist) that houses my *spirit* during my manifested *finite* flesh existence. My *flesh* will vanish (die) – my *spirit* will live on (not die). My *infinite spirit* lives on either in eternal peace and happiness or in eternal pain – depending upon whether I overcome or succumb to *flesh* desires – depending upon whether I follow or blaspheme the *Holy Spirit residing in me* during my *finite* existence.

Chapter 2
The COVENANTS

I, like so many, thought I understood this Covenant stuff. I knew something about an Old Covenant, but that applied to the Jews of the Old Testament. I knew something about a New Covenant, which was where Jesus died for my sins so that I would go to heaven if I did my part – if I confessed my mortal sins to a priest before I died – if I performed all the necessary works – if I wept in some aha moment of confession to others – if I rededicated – if I etc., etc.… I have since looked deep into God's Word and have come to a profound appreciation of the Covenants – it is truly a big deal. It is God's grace reaching far beyond what I had been taught.

God made two covenants.
The Old Covenant – between *infinite* God and *finite* Man.
The New Covenant – between *infinite* God and *infinite* Jesus.

————— ♦ —————

Acknowledging the Time Paradox is critical to understanding God's Word.

I have come to realize that accepting the Time Paradox of *"I am"* is critical to understanding God's Word and covenants.

God & Man Covenant
The Old Covenant

The old covenant promise is between God and Abraham and relies upon the strength, power and resolve of *finite* mortal priests and *finite* mortal men.

NKJV Scripture	NSECB Definitions
Hos 6:7. **"But like men they transgressed the covenant[1285]; There they dealt treacherously with Me**.	[1285]covenant. a compact (because made by passing between pieces of flesh): -confederacy, [con-] feder [-ate], covenant, league.

In the old covenant, God's promise is conditional upon *finite* men performing their part. The above cited scripture reveals the inability of men to keep the old covenant.

God & Jesus Covenant
The New Covenant

The new covenant is between God and Jesus. In the new covenant, God's promise is conditional upon the *infinite* Jesus performing and mediating what had been *finite* man's part in the old covenant.

The following scriptures reveal (i) the *forever* covenant between God and Jesus, (ii) Jesus as the *forever* priest mediator for each of us, and (iii) the Holy Spirit's *one-on-one teaching* directly to each of us.

NKJV Scripture	NSECB Definitions
Heb 7:20-22. And inasmuch as He was not made priest without an oath (for they have become priests without an oath, but He with an oath by Him who said to Him: "The LORD has sworn And will not relent, **'You are a priest forever**[0165] According to the order of Melchizedek'"**), by so much more **Jesus has become a surety of a better covenant.**	[0093]**unrighteousness.** injustice (properly, the quality, by implication, the act); morally, wrongfulness (of character, life or act).
Heb 7:28. For **the law appoints as high priests men who have weakness, but the word of the oath, which came after the law, appoints the Son who has been perfected forever**[0165].	[0165]**forever.** properly, an age; by extension, perpetuity (also past); by implication, the world; specially (Jewish) a Messianic period (present or future).
Heb 8:6. But now He has obtained a more excellent ministry, inasmuch as **He is also Mediator**[3316] **of a better covenant, which was established on better promises**.	[0379]**without excuse.** indefensible. [1242]**covenant.** properly, a disposition, i.e. (specially) a contract (especially a devisory will).
Heb 8:7-12. For if that first covenant[9999] had been faultless, then no place would have been sought for a second. Because finding fault with them, He says: "Behold, the days are coming, says the LORD, when **I will make a new**[2537] **covenant**[1242] **with the house of Israel and with the house of Judah** – not according to the covenant[1242] that I made with their fathers in the day when I took them by the hand to lead them out of the land of Egypt; because they did not continue in My covenant[1242], and I disregarded them, says the LORD. For this is the covenant[1242] that I will make with the house of Israel after those days, says the LORD: **I will put My laws in their mind**[1271] **and write them on their hearts**[2588]**; and I will be their God, and they shall be My people. None of them shall teach his neighbor, and none his brother, saying, 'Know the LORD,' for all shall know Me, from the least of them to the greatest of them. For I will be merciful**[2436] **to their unrighteousness**[0093]**, and their sins and their lawless deeds I will remember**[3403] **no more."**	[1271]**minds.** deep thought, properly, the faculty (mind or its disposition), by implication, its exercise. [2436]**forgive.** cheerful (as attractive), i.e. propitious; adverbially (by Hebraism) God be gracious!, i.e. (in averting some calamity) far be it. [2529]**are clearly seen.** to behold fully, i.e.(figuratively)distinctly apprehend. [2537]**new.** of uncertain affinity; new. especially in freshness. [2588]**hearts.** prolonged from a primary kar (Latin, cor, "heart"); the heart, i.e. (figuratively) the thoughts or feelings (mind); also (by analogy) the middle. [3316]**mediator.** a go-between, i.e. (simply) an internunciator, or (by implication) a reconciler (intercessor). [3403]**remember.** to remind, i.e. (middle voice) to recall to mind.
Rom 1:20-21. For since the creation of the world **His invisible attributes are clearly seen**[2529], being understood by the things that are made, even His eternal power and Godhead, so that they are **without excuse**[0379], because, although they knew God, they did not glorify Him as God, nor were thankful, but became futile in their thoughts, and their foolish hearts were darkened.	[9999]Inserted Word: not in the original Greek.

The first covenant between God and our forefathers did not work very well. God was faithful in his promise, but mankind was not faithful to God. In the first covenant, God delivered his people and spoke to them through patriarchs and prophets such as Moses. The problem was the people's performance was reliant upon *finite* mortal priests from the tribe of Levi and upon *finite* mortal people following God's laws. Since the first covenant was not working, God declared *"I will make a new covenant with the house of Israel and with the house of Judah".* Heb 8:8

In this new covenant, God declared *"I will put My laws in their mind and write them on their hearts; and I will be their God, and they shall be My people. None of them shall teach his neighbor, and none his brother, saying, 'Know the LORD,' for all shall know Me, from the least of them to the greatest of them. For I will be merciful to their unrighteousness, and their sins and their lawless deeds I will remember no more."* Heb 8:10

———— ◆ ————

As I contemplate the Time Paradox and the *infinite "I am"*, I see the pure grace new covenant manifested to us in *finite* time.

- **The *infinite* Jesus replaced *finite* man as the permanent mediator between God and man** Heb 7:20-22 & 28.
- **God promised to speak directly to the hearts and minds of His people, rather than through patriarchs and prophets** Heb 8:10 **(i.e., rather than through modern day priests, preachers and prophets).**
- **God puts His truth directly into every man's heart so that men are "without excuse".** Rom 1:20

Jesus the Final Sacrifice and Only Mediator

There is no shortage of words in the Christian belief that Jesus died for our sins. What is not so common, however, is a full appreciation of the breadth of Jesus' sacrifice. Jesus sacrificed Himself for *all (no one is excluded)*.

NKJV Scripture	NSECB Definitions
John 1:11-13. He came to His own, and His own did not receive Him. **But as many as received[2983] Him, to them He gave the right[1849] to become[1096] children[5043] of God, to those who believe in His name:** who were **born[1080], not of blood, nor of the will of the flesh, nor of the will of man, but of God.**	[1080]**born.** to procreate (properly, of the father, but by extension of the mother); figuratively, to regenerate. [1096]**to become.** a prolongation and middle voice form of a primary verb; to cause to be ("gen"- erate), i.e. (reflexively) to become (come into being), used with great latitude. [1849]**right.** privilege, i.e. (subjectively) force, capacity, competency, freedom, or (objectively) mastery (concretely, magistrate, superhuman, potentate, token of control), delegated influence. KJV: authority, jurisdiction, liberty, power, right, strength. [2983]**received.** a prolonged form of a primary verb, which is use only as an alternate in certain tenses; to take [properly objective or active, to get hold of; whereas 1209 is rather subjective or passive, to have offered to one; while 138 is more violent, to seize or remove]). [5043]**children.** a child (as produced).

John 1:11-13 sets the stage – although Jesus came to His own [Jews] and was rejected, God's gift is extended to *all who believe and receive*. In John 1:11-13, the emphasis is *not on me receiving – the emphasis is on Jesus giving*. In too many religious venues the primary emphasis is *improperly* focused on my believing and receiving to gain status as an heir of God. The confusion stems from the wording of John 1:12 which can be misleading with the words *"**right to become children** of God"*. The Greek interlinear and expanded definitions reads *"**power sons of God, to become**"* as follows.

Greek Interlinear	LaForge Commentary Definitions
John 1:12. as many as But received Him, gave He to them **power**[1849] **sons**[5043] of God, **to become**[1096] to them that believe on name His.	[1849]**power.** *eksousia* denotes authority or conferred power operating in a designated jurisdiction – the authority God gives to His children authorizing them to act to the extent they are guided by faith. [5043]**sons.** *teknon* denotes a child living in full dependence on the heavenly Father, i.e. fully relying upon the Lord in glad submission. [1096]**to become.** *ginomai* means to emerge or transition from one condition to another – to come into being implying motion and growth.

The underlying Greek meaning for the words in John 1:12, reveal the true meaning of John 1:12. The emphasis is <u>*not on me*</u> *becoming a child of God* – the emphasis is <u>*on Jesus*</u> giving me *eksousia authority* as a *teknon child* of God for my *ginomai growth*. As I reach the age of understanding, my believing and receiving is definitely required. Commensurate with my truly believing and submitting to Jesus, He grants me *birthright* power and authority as one of His children – no one is excluded.

———— ◆ ————

In the preceding study of John 1:11-13, I learn about the all-inclusive nature of God's gift through Jesus. In John 14:6, I also learn that Jesus is the *only* way – *no one* comes to the Father except through Jesus. 1Tim 2:3-6 confirms that (i) our Savior wants *all men* to be saved and know the truth, and (ii) Jesus is the *sole* mediator between God and man.

NKJV Scripture	NSECB Definitions
John 14:6. Jesus said to him, "I am the **way**[3598], the truth, and the **life**[2222]. No one comes to the Father except **through**[1223] Me."	[0444]**men.** man-faced, i.e. a human being. [1223]**through.** primary preposition denoting the channel of an act; through (in very wide applications, local, causal, or occasional). [1922]**knowledge.** recognition, i.e. (by implication) full discernment, acknowledgement. [2222]**life.** life (literally or figuratively. [3316]**mediator.** a go-between, i.e. (simply) an internunciator, or (by implication) a reconciler (intercessor). [3598]**way.** apparently a primary word; a road; by implication a progress (the route, act or distance); figuratively, a mode or means. [3956]**all, all things.** including all the forms of declension; apparently a primary word; all, any, every, the whole.
1Tim 2:3-6. For this is good and acceptable in the sight of **God our Savior, who desires all**[3956] **men**[0444] **to be saved and to come to the knowledge**[1922] **of the truth. For there is one God and one Mediator**[3316] **between God and men, the Man Christ Jesus, who gave Himself a ransom for all**[3956], to be testified in due time,	

The following scriptures are additional testimony that the primary emphasis is about *Jesus giving* – about Jesus as the *final sacrifice* and the *sole mediator* for *all mankind*.

NKJV Scripture	NSECB Definitions
Rom 5:10-11. For if when we were enemies we were reconciled[2644] to God through the death of His Son, much more, having been reconciled[2644], we shall be saved[4982] by His life. And not only that, but **we also rejoice in God through our Lord Jesus Christ, through whom we have now received the reconciliation[2643].**	[0266]**sin.** a sin (properly abstract); to miss the mark, i.e., to err. [0444]**men.** man-faced, i.e. a human being. [0458]**lawless.** illegality, i.e. violation of law or (genitive case) wickedness. [0859]**remission.** freedom; (figuratively) pardon. [0915]**barbarian.** of uncertain derivation; a foreigner (i.e. non-Greek).
Col 1:19-20. For it pleased the Father that in Him *[Jesus]* all the fullness should dwell, **and by[1223] Him *[Jesus]* to reconcile all things[3956] to Himself *[God]*, by Him *[Jesus]*, whether things on earth or things in heaven, having made peace through the blood of His cross.**	[1223]**by.** a primary preposition denoting the channel of an act; through (in very wide applications, local, causal, or occasional). [1242]**covenant.** properly, a disposition, i.e. (specially) a contract (especially a devisory will). [1401]**slave.** a slave (literal or figurative, involuntary or voluntary; frequently, therefore in a qualified sense of subjection or subserviency).
Col 3:11-12. where **there is neither Greek nor Jew, circumcised nor uncircumcised, barbarian[0915], Scythian[4658], slave[1401] nor free[1658], but Christ is all[3956] and in all[3956].** Therefore, as the elect[1588] of God, holy and beloved, put on tender mercies, kindness, humility, meekness, longsuffering;	[1588]**elect.** select; by implication, favorite. [1658]**free.** unrestrained (to go at pleasure), i.e. (as a citizen) not a slave (whether freeborn or manumitted), or (genitive case) exempt (from obligation or liability). [2511]**purify.** to cleanse (literally or figuratively). [2537]**new.** of uncertain affinity; new. especially in freshness.
Titus 2:11-14. **For the grace of God that brings salvation[4992] has appeared to all[3956] men[0444],** teaching us that, denying ungodliness and worldly lusts, we should live soberly, righteously, and godly in the present age, looking for the blessed hope and glorious appearing of our great **God and Savior Jesus Christ, who gave Himself for us, that He might redeem[3084] us from every[3956] lawless[0458] deed and purify[2511] for Himself His own special people[2992], zealous for good works.**	[2643]**reconciliation.** exchange (figuratively, adjustment), i.e. restoration to (the divine) favor. [2644]**reconciled.** to change mutually, i.e. (figuratively) to compound a difference. [2817]**inheritance.** heirship, i.e. (concretely) a patrimony or (genitive case) a possession. [2992]**people.** apparently a primary word; a people (in general; thus differing from 1218, which denotes one's own populace). [3084]**redeem.** to ransom (literally or figuratively). [3316]**mediator.** a go-between, i.e. (simply) an internunciator, or (by implication) a reconciler (intercessor).
Heb 9:14-15. how much more shall the blood of Christ, who through the eternal Spirit offered Himself without spot to God, **cleanse your conscience from dead works to serve the living God? And for this reason He is the Mediator[3316] of the new[2537] covenant[1242], by means of death, for the redemption of the transgressions[3847] under the first[4413] covenant[1242], that those who are called may receive the promise of the eternal inheritance[2817].**	[3403]**remember.** to remind, i.e. (middle voice) to recall to mind. [3847]**transgressions.** Violation [3956]**all, all things.** including all the forms of declension; apparently a primary word; all, any, every, the whole. [4376]**offering.** presentation; concretely, an oblation (bloodless) or sacrifice. [4413]**first.** foremost (in time, place, order or importance). [4658]**Scythian.** probably of foreign origin; a Scythene or Scythian, i.e. (by implication) a savage.
Heb 10:17-18. then He adds, **"Their sins and their**	[4982]**we shall be saved.** from a primary sos (contraction

lawless deeds I will remember[3403] **no more." Now where there is remission**[0859] **of these, there is no longer an offering**[4376] **for sin**[0266]**.**

for *cleanse* saoz, "safe"); to save, i.e. deliver or protect (literally or figuratively).
[4992]salvation. defender or (by implication) defense.

———— ◆ ————

Our study of God's Word confirms the basic tenant of most theologies is that Jesus died for my sins. Jesus gave himself to *cleanse* my conscience from acts that lead to death. There is no need for any more sacrifices – *infinite* Jesus is the final sacrifice for the forgiveness of sins. Jesus, as the sole mediator of the new covenant, is the only way to the Father.

However, what is not so common is a grasp in the all-inclusive scope of the new covenant. The new covenant promise covers *all of mankind*. The Word makes it very clear that *all of mankind* is included with the words ***"there is neither Greek nor Jew, circumcised nor uncircumcised, barbarian, Scythian, slave nor free, but Christ is all and in all"***. *Col 3:11*

Now for the almost unbelievable – the new covenant is a pure grace covenant – a pure gift from God – neither part of the covenant is reliant upon *mortal* man's fulfillment. The first covenant *law* appoints men as high priests who are both mortal and weak. The new covenant oath *fulfills the law* and appoints Jesus as the permanent high priest mediator between God and me. Jesus offered Himself to *cleanse* our consciences from acts that lead to death. Jesus offered Himself as a ransom for *all* mankind. Jesus offered Himself as the *final* sacrifice for the forgiveness of the sins of *all* mankind. Jesus is the eternal mediator between God and me.

> **God fulfills one part of the covenant.**
> **Jesus fulfills the other part of the covenant.**
> **Jesus gave himself as a ransom for *all mankind*.**
> **My part is to believe, receive and live the gift.**
> **I am a pure *grace* recipient.**

Chapter 3
BORN AGAIN

There was a time when I thought *born again* talk was a bit overly pious...
... I again had to remap my thinking.

I had to tackle the big question – when "did or does" the new covenant promise *to each of us* take effect regarding (i) my being righteousness through the blood of Jesus and (ii) my inheritance of eternal life through the resurrection of Jesus? I learned that the new covenant promise took effect for me when the Lamb was slain from the foundation [creation] of the world. *Rev 13:8*.

As I mentioned in **Chapter 1, The Time Paradox,** Jesus' covenant death and resurrection for the sins of all mankind was fulfilled before man's *finite flesh* came into being and before man's *finite* world was born – i.e., *"All who dwell on the earth will worship him, whose names have not been written in the Book of Life of the Lamb slain from the foundation [creation] of the world." Rev 13:8*

Predominate Christian teaching is that I must be born again to be saved – this statement is simple truth. However, most of the doctrinal reality I have experienced adds to the simple truth and goes on to intertwine a cloaked Christian teaching of saved by grace, but only if adequately supplemented with altar calls, sin management, confessions and good works to attain the *born again saved* status.

Some teach that if I am a born again saved individual, that I cannot lose my salvation. Recently I heard an individual boast that he was saved and that the proof was that he did not sin anymore (the statement itself may have been a manifestation of 1John 1:8). The logic was that if I am still capable of sin, then I simply am not a born again saved individual – logic akin to false circular reasoning.

Some teach that all are born with the imputed sin of Adam, but if a child dies before saying the sinner's prayer, God will ignore the sin because the children are innocent. This theology conveys that God can live with the imputed sin of a child but not the imputed sin of an adult. If true, then at what age does an innocent saved child become a lost sinner in need of being re-saved?

As I mentioned earlier, the truth is really quite simple. God and Jesus have a new covenant promise to *all* of mankind – I have no say in the promise. This new covenant is a pure grace covenant between God and Jesus. I am a beneficiary of the new covenant – I do not earn (but can reject) eternal life with Jesus.

In this chapter, I look directly to the Word to comprehend *born again*, the *grace* of God, the *resurrection* of Jesus and the *shepherding* of the Holy Spirit.

Born Again Defined

John 3:3-15 summarizes the definition of *born again*.

- **My first birth is my flesh birth – as a descendant of Adam and Eve.**
- **Born again is my spiritual birth – inheritance through Jesus resurrection.**

Born again is not a feeling – Born again is *not* a status I achieve – it's *not* about me – it is *not* about something I do. Born again is about Jesus – it is my grace inheritance – it is God's gift to me through Jesus.

NKJV Scripture	NSECB Definitions
John 3:3-15. Jesus answered and said to him, Most assuredly, I say to you, **unless one is born[1080] again[0509], he cannot see the kingdom of God.** Nicodemus said to Him, How can a man be born when he is old? Can he enter a second time into his mother's womb and be born? Jesus answered, Most assuredly, I say to you, **unless one is born[1080] of water[5204] and the Spirit[4151], he cannot enter[1525] the kingdom of God. That which is born[1080] of the flesh[4561] is flesh[4561], and that which is born[1080] of the Spirit[4151] is spirit[4151].** Do not marvel that I said to you, 'You must be born[1080] again[0509].' **The wind blows where it wishes, and you hear the sound of it, but cannot tell where it comes from and where it goes. So is everyone who is born[1080] of the Spirit[4151].** Nicodemus answered and said to Him, How can these things be? Jesus answered and said to him, Are you the teacher of Israel, and do not know these things? Most assuredly, I say to you, We speak what We know and testify what We have seen, and you do not receive Our witness. If I have told you earthly things and you do not believe, how will you believe if I tell you heavenly things? No one has ascended to heaven but He who came down from heaven, that is[9999], the Son of Man who is in heaven[9999]. And as Moses lifted up the serpent in the wilderness, **even so must the Son of Man be lifted up, that whoever believes in Him** should not perish but[9999] **have eternal life[2222].**	[0509]**again.** from above; by analogy, from the first; by implication, anew. [1080]**born.** to procreate (properly, of the father, but by extension of the mother); figuratively, to regenerate. [1525]**enter.** to enter (literally or figuratively). [2222]**life.** life (literally or figuratively). [4151]**spirit.** a current of air, i.e. breath (blast) or a breeze; by analogy or figuratively, a spirit, i.e. (human) the rational soul, (by implication) vital principle, mental disposition, etc., or (superhuman) an angel, demon, or (divine) God, Christ's spirit, the Holy Spirit. [4561]**flesh.** flesh (as stripped of the skin), i.e. (strictly) the meat of an animal (as food), or (by extension) the body (as opposed to the soul [or spirit], or as the symbol of what is external, or as the means of kindred), or (by implication) human nature (with its frailties [physically or morally] and passions), or (specifically) a human being (as such). [5204]**water.** water (as if rainy) literally or figuratively. [9999]. Inserted words; not in the original Greek.

John 3:3-15 Jesus teaches us four major principles regarding *born again*.
- **No one can enter the kingdom of God unless he is born again.** *John 3:3*
- **Flesh gives birth to flesh (first birth).** *John 3:6*
- **Spirit gives birth to spirit (second birth – *born again*).** *John 3:6*
- ***Born again* is being *born of the Spirit*.** *John 3:7*

In John 3:14-15, Jesus also teaches us *"even so must the Son of Man be lifted up, that whoever believes in Him have eternal life"*. In these words we have direct reference to being born again through Jesus' resurrection.

———— ♦ ————

Concurring with Jesus' teachings in John 3:3-15, the 1Peter 1:3-5 and 1Peter 1:23 teachings read as follows.

NKJV Scripture	NSECB Definitions
LaForge Commentary. In the following verses, 1Peter 1:3-5 is translated **has begotten us again**[0313], whereas 1Peter 1:23 is translated **have been born again**[0313]. It is crucial for us to recognize that **has begotten again**[0313] & **born again**[0313] are from the same Greek word and carry the same meaning.	
1 Peter 1:3-5. Blessed be the God and Father of our Lord Jesus Christ, who according to His abundant mercy **has begotten us again**[0313] **to a living hope through**[1223] **the resurrection**[0386] **of Jesus Christ from the dead**[3498], to an inheritance[2817] incorruptible and undefiled and that does not fade away, reserved in heaven for you, who are kept by the power of God through faith for salvation ready to be revealed in the last time.	[0313]**has begotten again, born again.** to beget or (by extension) bear (again). [0386]**resurrection.** a standing up again, i.e. (literally) a resurrection from death (individual, genitive case or by implication [its author]), or (figuratively) a (moral) recovery (of spiritual truth). [1223]**through.** a primary preposition denoting the channel of an act; through (in very wide applications, local, causal, or occasional). [2198]**lives.** a primary verb; to live (literally or figuratively). [2817]**inheritance.** heirship, i.e. (concretely) a patrimony or (genitive case) a possession. [3056]**word.** something said (including the thought); by implication a topic (subject of discourse), also reasoning (the mental faculty) or motive; by extension, a computation; specifically (with the article in John) the Divine Expression (i.e. Christ).
1 Peter 1:23. **having been born again**[0313], **not of corruptible seed but incorruptible, through**[1223] **the word**[3056] **of God which lives**[2198] **and abides**[3306] **forever,**	[3306]**abides.** a primary verb; to stay (in a given place, state, relation or expectancy). [3498]**dead.** from an apparently primary nekus (a corpse); dead (literally or figuratively; also as noun).

1Peter 1:3-5 is summarily emphatic: ***"...has begotten us again to a living hope through the resurrection of Jesus Christ from the dead..."*** The language is clear in that I have been given a **new birth (born again) by the resurrection of Jesus**, not by something I do or say.

1Peter 1:23 continues with ***"having been born again, not of corruptible seed but incorruptible, through the word of God which lives and abides forever..."*** The language is again clear – I have been given a **new birth (born again) through the Word [Jesus]**, not by something I do or say.

———— ◆ ————

When I read John 3:3-15, 1Peter 1:3 and 1Peter 1:23 in their proper context, I learn that born again status is not something I attain – I have no say in the matter. Born again status is not about me having an aha moment where my belief works are rewarded and I precipitously become a born again saved person. While many people do experience a memorable aha moment that turns them from the gravities of insurrection, the moment does not somehow earn them born again status.

The proper focus belongs on Jesus – on ***"the Lamb slain from the foundation [creation] of the world"*** [Rev 13:8] – on Jesus attaining my born again status for me through His resurrection in the Word. In John 3:3-15, Jesus is teaching

Nicodemus about grace salvation through Jesus and the Word. Jesus is prophesying about why He must suffer in death and prevail in resurrection – so that I can be born again and can see the kingdom of God. Quite simply, I am a beneficiary of born again status at the moment of my conception – it is God's gift.

Jesus Is the Firstborn

Looking further into scripture, we confirm that Jesus Himself is the firstborn from the dead. The manifested Jesus was first born of the flesh – His first birth. The manifested Jesus was *born again* (His *spiritual birth*) at His resurrection from His flesh death.

NKJV Scripture	NSECB Definitions
Col 1:13-18. He has delivered us from the power of darkness and conveyed us into the kingdom of the Son of His love, in whom we have redemption through His blood, the forgiveness of sins. **He is the image of the invisible God, the firstborn[4416] over all[3956] creation[2937].** For by Him all things were created that are in heaven and that are on earth, visible and invisible, whether thrones or dominions or principalities or powers. **All[3956] things were created[2936] through Him and for Him.** And He is before all things, and in Him all things consist. And He is the head of the body, the church, **who is the beginning[0746], the firstborn[4416] from the dead[3498]**, that in all things He may have the preeminence.	[0746]**beginning.** (properly abstract) a commencement, or (concretely) chief (in various applications of order, time, place, or rank). [0932]**kings.** properly, royalty, i.e. (abstractly) rule, or (concretely) a realm (literally or figuratively). [2409]**priests.** a priest (literally or figuratively). [2936]**created.** probably akin to 2932 (through the idea of proprietor-ship of the manufacturer); to fabricate, i.e. found (form originally). [2937]**creation.** original formation (properly, the act; by implication, the thing, literally or figuratively). [3498]**dead.** from an apparently primary nekus (a corpse); dead (literally or figuratively; also as noun).
Rev 1:5-6. and from **Jesus Christ, the faithful witness, the firstborn[4416] from the dead[3498]**, and the ruler over the kings of the earth. To Him who loved us and washed us from our sins in His own blood, **and has made us kings[0932] and priests[2409] to His God and Father**, to Him be glory and dominion forever and ever. Amen.	[3956]**all.** including all the forms of declension; apparently a primary word; all, any, every, the whole. [4416]**firstborn.** first-born (usually as noun, literally or figuratively).

Scripture is clear – Jesus is the firstborn from the dead.

- **Jesus is the beginning and the firstborn from among the dead.** *Col 1:18*
- **Jesus is the firstborn from the dead.** *Rev 1:5*
- **Jesus is the firstborn over all creation.** *Col 1:15*

For All Mankind

Looking further, we continue to learn that Jesus is the firstborn for *all mankind*. No one is mentioned as being excluded

NKJV Scripture	NSECB Definitions
1Cor 15:20-22. But now Christ is risen from the dead, and has become the first fruits of those who have fallen asleep. For since by man came death, by Man also	[0386]**resurrection.** from 450; a standing up again, i.e. (literally) a resurrection from death (individual, genitive case or by implication [its author]), or

came the resurrection[0386] of the dead[3498]. **For as in Adam all[3956] die, even so in Christ all[3956]** *shall be*** **made alive[2227].**

LaForge Commentary. The translation insertion of *shall* be** conveys a misleading futuristic context. This Greek form is passive context "to make alive", "I make that which was dead to live", "cause to live", "give life", "quicken."

Gal 3:28. There is neither Jew nor Greek, there is neither slave nor free, **there is neither male nor female; for you are all one in Christ Jesus.**

Gal 4:7. Therefore **you are no longer a slave[1401] but a son[5207], and if a son, then an heir[2818] of God through Christ.**

LaForge Commentary. Translations of **son[5207]** from Greek to English include "child" and "foal" and include both male and female. **References to "child/son/heir" of God include male & female.**

(figuratively) a (moral) recovery (of spiritual truth).

[1401]slave. from 1210; a slave (literal or figurative, involuntary or voluntary; frequently, therefore in a qualified sense of subjection or subserviency).

[2227]alive. to (re-) vitalize (literally or figuratively).

[2818]heir. from 2819 and the base of 3551 (in its original sense of partitioning, i.e. [reflexively] getting by apportionment); a sharer by lot, i.e. inheritor (literally or figuratively); by implication, a possessor.

[3498]dead. from an apparently primary nekus (a corpse); dead (literally or figuratively; also as noun).

[3956]all. including all the forms of declension; apparently a primary word; all, any, every, the whole.

[5207]son. apparently a primary word; a "son" (sometimes of animals), used very widely of immediate, remote or figuratively, kinship.

Scripture tells us *"For as in Adam all die, so in Christ all* shall be** *made alive."* [1Cor15:22] I see a pivotal element in Paul's writings.

The words *"...all die"* and *"...all made alive"* means *all* – no one is excluded. Again, the translation insertion of shall be** conveys a misleading futuristic context. When properly translated, the scripture verse has a compelling tit-for-tat language structure – *as in Adam all die so in Christ all made alive.*

Scripture also tells us *"there is neither male nor female; for you are all one in Christ Jesus"* [Gal 3:28] and *"you are no longer a slave but a son, and if a son, then an heir of God through Christ"* [Gal 4:7].

———— ◆ ————

While still alive on the cross, Jesus gave us a critical revelation that is rarely mentioned in religious teachings. Forgiveness does *not require* confessions to others, repeated alter calls, grieved emotions and other displays of human works. However, on the other hand, if I unashamedly reject Jesus and blaspheme the Holy Spirit in me, I forfeit my inheritance.

NKJV Scripture	LaForge Commentary
Luke 23:32-34. There were also two others, criminals, led with Him to be put to death. And when they had come to the place called Calvary, there they crucified Him, and the criminals, one on the right hand and the other on the left. **Then Jesus said, "Father, forgive them, for they do not know what they do." And they divided His garments and cast lots.**	*Commentary.* Jesus spoke forgiveness for the very ones casting lots for his clothing – simply citing that **they know not what they do** – their asking for forgiveness was not a prerequisite.
Luke 23:39-43. Then one of the criminals who were hanged blasphemed Him, saying, "If You are the Christ, save Yourself and us." But **the other, answering, rebuked him, saying, "Do**	*Commentary.* The one criminal appears to commit the sin of blasphemy against the **Holy Spirit**

you not even fear God, seeing you are under the same condemnation? And we indeed justly, for we receive the due reward of our deeds; but this Man has done nothing wrong." Then he said to Jesus, "**Lord, remember me when You come into Your kingdom.**" And Jesus said to him, "**Assuredly, I say to you, today you will be with Me in Paradise.**"

residing in him – the unforgivable sin. I discuss this kind of blasphemy in Chapter on Overcoming.

While Jesus was hanging on the cross, he prayed *"Father, forgive them, for they do not know what do."* [Luke 23:34] and *"Assuredly, I say to you, today you will be with Me in Paradise."* [Luke 23:43]. I see several pivotal elements in Jesus' prayers.

- Jesus' *finite flesh* manifestation of His *sacrificial death* on the cross had *not* yet occurred.
- Jesus' mediation for *all* included the execution soldiers *without* them first asking for forgiveness.
- *Requesting* forgiveness for my sins is *not* a prerequisite.
- Forgiveness *includes all* mankind.
- Jesus' pleading for his crucifiers *because* *"they do not know what they do"*.
- Jesus' promise to the accepting, believing and submitting criminal *"today you will be with Me in paradise"*.
- Jesus will leave me hanging if I blaspheme the Holy Spirit residing in me.

The Book of Life

While researching the *Time Paradox*, the *Covenants* and *Born Again*, I noted a recurring reference to a *book of life*. Both the Old and New Testaments reference a *book of life* belonging to the Lamb slain from the foundation [creation] of the world – an aspect of the *Time Paradox*. The *book of life* is rarely mentioned in religious circles or Sunday classes; however, scripture tells us the following.

The *book of life* contains names written since the creation of the world.
The *book of life* is akin to a guest list for eternal life with Jesus.
My cleansing and forgiveness *preceded* Jesus' *manifested* flesh death.
If I blaspheme the Holy Spirit residing in me I will be blotted out of the *book*.
Anyone not written in the *book of life* is thrown into the lake of fire.
Anyone not written in the *book of life* cannot enter into eternal life with Jesus.

The *book of life* is a big deal; direct scripture references include the following.

NKJV Scripture (Old Testament)	NSECB Definitions
Exo 32:31-35. Then Moses returned to the LORD and said, "Oh, these people have committed a great sin, and have made for themselves a god of gold! **Yet now, if You will forgive their sin — but if not, I pray, blot me**[4229] **out of Your book**[5612] **which You have written**[3789]**."** **And the LORD said to Moses, "Whoever has sinned against Me, I will blot**[4229] **him out of My book**[5612]. Now therefore, go, lead the people to the place of which I have spoken to you. Behold, My Angel shall go before	[2416]living. alive; hence, raw (flesh); fresh (plant, water, year), strong; also (as noun, especially in the feminine singular and masculine plural) life (or living thing), whether literally or figuratively. [3789]written. A primitive root; to grave, by implication, to write (describe, inscribe, prescribe, subscribe). [4229]blot, blotted. A primitive root;

you. Nevertheless, in the day when I visit for punishment, I will visit punishment upon them for their sin." So the LORD plagued the people because of what they did with the calf which Aaron made.

Psa 69:27-28. Add iniquity to their iniquity, And let them not come into Your righteousness. **Let them be blotted[4229] out of the book[5612] of the living[2416], And not be written[3789] with the righteous[6662].**

properly, to stroke or rub; by implication, to erase; also to smooth (as if with oil), i.e. grease or make fat; also to touch, i.e. reach to.
[5612]**book**. properly, writing (the art or a document); by implication, a book.
[6662]**righteous**. to be right in a moral or forensic sense.

NKJV Scripture (New Testament)	NSECB Definitions
Phlp 4:2-3. I implore Euodia and I implore Syntyche to be of the same mind in the Lord. And I urge you also, true companion, help these women who labored with me in the gospel, with Clement also, **and the rest of my fellow workers[4904], whose names[3868] are in the Book[0976] of Life[2222].**	[0455]**opened**. to open up (literally or figuratively, in various applications. [0721]**Lamb, Lamb's**. a lambkin. [0975]**book**. a roll. [0976]**book**. Properly, the inner bark of the papyrus plant, i.e. (by implication) a sheet or scroll of writing.
Rev 3:5. He who overcomes shall be clothed in white garments, and I will not blot out[1813] his name[3686] from[1537] the Book[0976] of Life[2222]; but I will confess his name before My Father and before His angels.	[1125]**written**. A primary verb; to "grave", especially to write; figuratively, to describe. [1536]**anyone's**. if any.
Rev 13:8. **All who dwell on the earth will worship him, whose names[3686] have not been written[1125] in[1722] the Book[0975] of Life[2222] of the Lamb[0721] slain from the foundation[2602] of the world[2889].**	[1537]**from**. A primary preposition denoting origin (the point whence action or motion proceeds), from, out (of place, time, or cause; literal or figurative; direct or remote).
Rev 17:8. ...whose names[3686] are not written[1125] in the Book[0975] of Life[2222] from the foundation[2602] of the world[2889], when they see the beast that was, and is not, and yet is.	[1722]**in**. A primary preposition denoting (fixed) position (in place, time or state). [1813]**blot out**. to smear out, i.e. obliterate (erase tears, figuratively, pardon sin).
Rev 20:12-15. And I saw the dead, small and great, standing before God, and books were opened. **And another book[0975] was opened[0455], which is the Book of Life[2222].** And the dead were judged according to their works, by the things which were written in the books. The sea gave up the dead who were in it, and Death and Hades delivered up the dead who were in them. And they were judged, each one according to his works. **Then Death and Hades were cast into the lake of fire. This is the second death. And anyone[1536] not found[2147] written[1125] in the Book[0976] of Life[2222] was cast into the lake of fire.**	[2147]**found**. A prolonged form of a primary heuro (hyoo'-ro); which (together with another cognate form heureo (hyoo-reh'-o)) is used for it in all the tenses except the present and imperfect; to find (literally or figuratively). [2222]**life**. life (literally or figuratively). [2602]**foundation**. a deposition, i.e. founding; figuratively, conception.
Rev 21:10. And he carried me away in the Spirit to a great and high mountain, and showed me the great city, **the holy Jerusalem, descending out of heaven from God...** **Rev 21:22-27**. But I saw no temple in it, **for the Lord God Almighty and the Lamb are its temple. The city had no need of the sun or of the moon to shine in it, for the glory of God illuminated it. The Lamb is its light.** And the nations of those who are saved shall walk in its light, and the kings of the earth bring their glory and honor into it. Its gates shall not be shut at all by day (there shall be no night there). And they shall bring the glory and the honor of the nations into it. **But there shall by no means enter it anything that defiles, or causes an abomination or a lie, but only those who are written[1125] in the Lamb's[0721] Book[0975] of Life[2222].**	[2889]**world**. orderly arrangement, i.e. decoration; by implication, the world (in a wide or narrow sense, including its inhabitants, literally or figuratively [morally]): [3686]**names, name**. a "name" (literally or figuratively) [authority, character]. [4904]**fellow workers**. a co-laborer, i.e. coadjutor. [4969]**slain**. A primary verb; to butcher (especially an animal for food or in sacrifice) or (generally) to slaughter, or (specifically) to maim (violently).

In the Old Testament, prior to Jesus' earthly manifestation and death on the cross, reference was made to a *book of life* by God, Moses and David. In the New Testament, after Jesus' earthly manifestation and death on the cross, reference was made to a *book of life* by Paul, John and Jesus.

God, Moses and David speak of actions where sinners and enemies could be *blotted out* of the *book of life* – with a knowledge that these people *are in the book of life*. *Exo 32:32 & Psa 69:28*

Paul simply speaks of his fellow workers with a knowledge that they *are in the book of life*. *Phlp 4:3*

In Revelations, Jesus affirms that those who overcome will *not be blotted out* of the Lamb's book of life that was *written at the creation of the world*. As for those who have been *blotted out* and not found in the book of life, their destiny is the second death (i.e., spiritual death). Jesus also speaks with knowledge that *those not blotted out* of the Lamb's book of life *are otherwise in the book of life*. *Rev 3:5, Rev 13:8, Rev 17:8, Rev 20:12 & Rev 21:27*

What are obvious are the references to a *book of life*. What is not so obvious is that God, Moses, David, Paul, John and Jesus all acknowledge that names are written in the *Lamb's Book of Life unless and until blotted out*. It is significant that no direct mention is made of when or how these people were first written into the *book of life* – their underlying assumption is simply that all are already in the *book of life*. A similar underlying assumption exists regarding the 100 sheep *Luke 15;4*, the 10 silver coins *Luke 15:8* and the 2 sons *Luke 15:11*.

So how "did or does" anyone, get written into this *book of life*? In Chapter 2, I discussed the new covenant agreement between God and Jesus **"For by Him [Jesus] all things were created that are in heaven and that are on earth, visible and invisible, whether thrones or dominions or principalities or powers. All things were created through Him [Jesus] and for Him [Jesus]"** *Col 1:16* When I look closely into scripture, I learn that I am born again solely by the mercy and grace of God – I can neither say nor do anything to achieve a born again status – *it's not about me, it's about Jesus*. Then, when I also consider the Time Paradox and the Lamb that was **"slain from the foundation [creation] of the world"** *Rev 13:8* I realize that *born again* is a birthright status. When I consider the **"book of life belonging to the Lamb slain from the foundation [creation] of the world"** *Rev 13:8* I realize that I am conceived in the *book of life* by virtue of my birthright *born again* status and that the *book of life* has been written from the foundation [creation] of the world.

———— ◆ ————

It is directly significant that when Paul is speaking to the gentiles, he makes multiple references to *what has already happened*, not *what will happen if...* The following scriptures are directly relevant to born again status and timing.

NKJV Scripture	NSECB Definitions

Eph 2:4-9. But God, who is rich in mercy, because of His great love with which He loved us, **even when we were dead[3498] in trespasses[3900], made us alive[4806] together with Christ (by grace you have been saved[4982]), and raised us up together**, and made us sit together in the heavenly places in Christ Jesus, that in the ages to come He might show the exceeding riches of His grace in His kindness toward us in Christ Jesus. **For by grace you have been saved[4982] through faith[4102], and that not of yourselves; it is the gift of God, not of works[2041], lest anyone should boast.**

Col 2:13-14. **And you, being dead[3498] in your trespasses[3900] and the uncircumcision of your flesh[4561], He [God] has made alive[4806] together with[4862] Him [Jesus], having forgiven you all trespasses, having wiped out the handwriting of requirements that was against us, which was contrary to us. And He [Jesus] has taken it out of the way, having nailed it to the cross.**

Col 2:20-3:4. **Therefore, if you died[0599] with Christ from the basic principles[4747] of the world[2889], why, as though living in the world, do you subject yourselves to regulations –** "Do not touch, do not taste, do not handle," which all concern things which perish with the using – according to the commandments and doctrines of men? These things indeed have an appearance of wisdom in self-imposed religion, false humility, and neglect of the body, but are of no value against the indulgence of the flesh. **If then you were raised[4891] with Christ, seek those things which are above, where Christ is, sitting at the right hand of God. Set your mind on things above, not on things on the earth. For you died[0599], and your life is hidden[2928] with Christ in God.** When Christ who is our life appears, then you also will appear with Him in glory.

Titus 3:4-7. But when the kindness and the love of God our Savior toward man appeared, not by works of righteousness which we have done, but according to His mercy **He saved[4982] us, through the washing[3067] of regeneration[3824] and renewing[0342] of the Holy Spirit[4151], whom He poured out on us abundantly through Jesus Christ our Savior, that having been justified[1344] by His grace we should become heirs according to the hope of eternal life.**

[0342]**renewal.** renovation.

[0599]**you died.** to die off (literally or figuratively).

[1344]**justified.** to render (i.e. show or regard as) just or innocent.

[2041]**works.** from a primary (but obsolete) ergo (to work); toil (as an effort or occupation); by implication, an act.

[2889]**world.** orderly arrangement, i.e. decoration; by implication, the world (in a wide or narrow sense, including its inhabitants, literally or figuratively [morally]).

[2928]**hidden.** a primary verb; to conceal (properly, by covering).

[3067]**washing.** a bath, i.e. (figuratively), immersion, baptism.

[3498]**dead.** from an apparently primary nekus (a corpse); dead (literally or figuratively; also as noun).

[3824]**regeneration.** (spiritual) rebirth (the state or the act), i.e. (figuratively) spiritual renovation; specifically, Messianic restoration.

[3900]**trespasses.** a side-slip (lapse or deviation), i.e. (unintentional) error or (willful) transgression.

[4102]**faith.** persuasion, i.e. credence; moral conviction (of religious truth, or the truthfulness of God or a religious teacher), especially reliance upon Christ for salvation; abstractly, constancy in such profession; by extension, the system of religious (Gospel) truth itself.

[4151]**Holy Spirit.** a current of air, i.e. breath (blast) or a breeze; by analogy or figuratively, a spirit, i.e. (human) the rational soul, (by implication) vital principle, mental disposition, etc., or (superhuman) an angel, demon, or (divine) God, Christ's spirit, the Holy Spirit.

[4561]**sinful nature.** flesh (as stripped of the skin), i.e. (strictly) the meat of an animal (as food), or (by extension) the body (as opposed to the soul [or spirit], or as the symbol of what is external, or as the means of kindred), or (by implication) human nature (with its frailties [physically or morally] and passions), or (specifically) a human being (as such).

[4747]**basic principles.** neuter of a presumed derivative of the base of 4748; something orderly in arrangement, i.e. (by implication) a serial (basal, fundamental, initial) constituent (literally), proposition (figuratively).

[4806]**God made you alive.** to reanimate conjointly with (figuratively).

[4862]**with.** a primary preposition denoting union; with or together (but much closer than 3326 or 3844), i.e. by association, companionship, process, resemblance, possession, instrumentality, addition, etc.

[4891]**raised.** to rouse (from death) in company with, i.e. (figuratively) to revivify (spiritually) in resemblance to:

[4982]**saved.** from a primary sos (contraction for obsolete saoz, "safe"); to save, i.e. deliver or protect (literally or figuratively).

It is significant that Paul's writings make known what has *already happened*.

- **Eph 2:4-9.** *when we were dead... made us alive... you have been saved...*
- **Col 2:13-14.** *being dead... He [God] has made alive...*
- **Col 2:20-3:3.** *you died with Christ... you were raised with Christ...*
- **Titus 3:4-7.** *He saved us... having been justified...*

Born Again Summary

God and Jesus made a new covenant promise to all of mankind – I had no say in the promise. The new covenant is a grace covenant – purely by the grace of God – a pure gift from God – my works add nothing. ^{Eph 2:8}

It is *earth-shattering and momentous* that Jesus, while still alive on the cross, forgave his crucifying persecutors without them first asking for forgiveness. ^{Luke 23:34} Am I to somehow expect Jesus has changed the rules for me? No. ***Jesus Christ is the same yesterday and today and forever***. ^{Heb 13:8} The answer is in the following parables by Jesus.

What man of you, having a hundred sheep, if he loses one of them, does not leave the ninety-nine in the wilderness, and go after the one which is lost until he finds it? ^{Luke 15:4} When and how did each of the sheep become part of the hundred? *Or what woman, having ten silver coins, if she loses one coin, does not light a lamp, sweep the house, and search carefully until she finds it?* ^{Luke 15:8} When and how did each of the coins become part of the ten? Jesus continued: *A certain man had two sons.* ^{Luke 15:11} When and how did the two sons become part of the family? The answer is in God's Word. ***He [Jesus] is the image of the invisible God, the firstborn over all creation. For by Him [Jesus] all things were created that are in heaven and that are on earth, visible and invisible, whether thrones or dominions or principalities or powers. All things were created through Him [Jesus] and for Him [Jesus].*** ^{Col 1:15-17} I belong to Jesus from my very conception. I am in the *book of life* at my very conception. I am conceived an heir of God.

Jesus further clarified with the following parable as he spoke directly to his disciples while calling a little child to stand among them and saying ***Then Jesus called a little child to Him, set him in the midst of them, and said, "Assuredly, I say to you, unless you are converted and become as little children, you will by no means enter the kingdom of heaven."*** ^{Matt 18:2-3} ***"Let the little children come to Me, and do not forbid them; for of such is the kingdom of God. Assuredly, I say to you, whoever does not receive the kingdom of God as a little child will by no means enter it."*** ^{Mark 10:14-15} Jesus would never instruct anyone to return to a child status (which many religious theologies teach lacks born again saved status) unless the real truth is that I am born into this *finite* world as a child/son/heir of God with all of the family rights to an *infinite* eternal life inheritance.

While dead in my sins and my flesh, God made me alive with Christ. ^{Col 2:13} I do not earn or pursue my way into eternal life with Jesus – I start there. *As a child I am born again.* I am born a child/son/heir of God with the inheritance of eternal life with Jesus. God saved me through the washing of rebirth and renewal by the Spirit (*born again*). *Titus 3:5* I am *born again* of imperishable seed [Jesus]. *1Pet 1:23* I am a birthright beneficiary of God's new covenant promise. *1Pet 1:3*

———— ♦ ————

John further teaches us *"If we confess our sins, he is faithful and just to forgive us our sins and to cleanse us from all unrighteousness".* *1John 1:9* Unfortunately, this verse is one of the most quoted yet most misunderstood verses in the bible.

- **"choice"** 1John 1:9 is all too often memorized and quoted by itself; however, verses 8, 9 & 10 must be read together. The concept is that I have a *choice* – *choice* can exist only with my understanding of the options. Verses 8, 9 & 10 all come into play as I grow in the continuum of my ability to make *free will choices.* Verses 8, 9 & 10 read as follows: *"If we say that we have no sin, we deceive ourselves, and the truth is not in us. If we confess our sins, He is faithful and just to forgive us our sins and to cleanse us from all unrighteousness. If we say that we have not sinned, we make Him a liar, and His word is not in us."*

- *"confess"* means to acknowledge and agree with Jesus that I am guilty of sin as charged. It does *not require* my confessions to others. The word *"confess"* appears in John 1:20, John 12:42, Romans 10:9, Philippians 2:11, Hebrews 3:1, Hebrews 13:15, James 5:16 and 1John 1:9. Confessing of *sin* is mentioned *only* in James 5:16 and 1John1:9 – in *all other* references confess relates to acknowledging and/or agreeing with Jesus.

- *"forgive"* means to send forth, or send away – as far as the east is from the west.

- *"cleanse"* means to *cleanse,* not *cover.* We are not *covered* by the blood – blood *covering* is an old covenant concept. In the new covenant, we are *cleansed* by the blood. Sadly, the popular hymn lyrics is just plain wrong.

With Jesus' words, I learn that if **I acknowledge and agree with Jesus that I sin by nature**, Jesus will **cast my sins away** and **cleanse** me from all unrighteousness. Jesus does *not require* confessions to others, repeated alter calls, grieved emotions and other displays of human works.

———— ♦ ————

As I enter the age of *understanding,* the free pass of innocent cleansed childhood expires. As I enter the age of *understanding,* I must now make a *mature free will choice* – ignore or listen – not believe or believe – reject or accept. *Rev 3:15* As I reach the age of *understanding,* I must mature by refocusing my belief, faith and trust from my earthly parents to full belief, faith and trust in Jesus (God has no grandchildren). It is my *free will choice* – I must either (i) choose my EGO spirit (**E**dge **G**od **O**ut) and blaspheme the Holy Spirit, or (ii) confess (*acknowledge and* *agree with Jesus*) that I need Jesus as my Lord and Savior. My part is to believe in Jesus and receive the gift. *All* who do not believe in Jesus stand condemned. *John 3:18* *All* who believe in Jesus have eternal life. *John 3:16*

As a birthright born again individual, I cannot *lose* my salvation but I can choose to *blaspheme* the Holy Spirit and *forfeit* my salvation. When I choose faith in Jesus, I preserve my eternal life inheritance – when I unashamedly reject Jesus and with resolve follow my *worldly flesh nature* (blaspheming the Holy Spirit), I forfeit my inheritance. *Blasphemy* against the Holy Spirit *residing in me* is the unforgiveable sin. *Matt 12:31, Mark 3:28 & Luke 12:10*

In the next chapter, I discuss *choices* and *overcoming* my flesh nature and looking forward to the inheritance that Jesus has already secured for me.

———— ◆ ————

PART II

Preserving My Birthright Inheritance

Chapter 4
OVERCOMING

In the Chapters 1 through 3, I delved into the simplicity of God's new covenant promise to each of us as a *child/son/heir of God.*

- **I begin my journey in the *book of life* as a *born again child/son/heir of God* with all the benefits of birthright eternal life inheritance.**
- **Then, as I reach the age of understanding, John 3:16 comes into play and I must mature by refocusing my belief, faith and trust from my earthly parents to a full belief, faith and trust in Jesus (God has no grandchildren).**

In Chapter 4, I delve into *preserving* my birthright inheritance – properly focusing my *free will choices* and *overcoming* my own EGO (**E**dge **G**od **O**ut) spirit.

- **Overcoming is about *avoiding* the EGO trap of *blaspheming* the Holy Spirit that resides in me (the unforgiveable sin).**
- **Overcoming is about *avoiding* the rebellion of a flesh vs spirit house divided against itself.**
- **Overcoming is about *not rejecting* my birthright inheritance.**
- **Overcoming is about hearing and following the guidance of the Holy Spirit that resides in me.**

Luke's account of the prodigal son is a parable of salvation – both sons were born in a family with all of the inheritance birthrights, but with the free will choice to reject life with the family. Facing the end, rather than remain lost forever, the prodigal son overcame his devastating *worldly flesh choices*, repented and returned to his family.

So what is my life all about – the big *why* – what is God doing? God desires an *eternal relationship* with His family. ***For the marriage of the Lamb has come, and His wife has made herself ready.*** **Rev 19:7** ***And I heard a loud voice from heaven saying, "Behold, the tabernacle of God is with men, and He will dwell with them, and they shall be His people. God Himself will be with them and be their God."*** **Rev 21:3** James teaches us about overcoming the competing worldly EGO spirit – ***Therefore submit to God. Resist the devil, and he will flee from you.*** **James 4:7** Peter also teaches – ***Be sober, be vigilant; because your adversary the devil walks about like a roaring lion, seeking whom he may devour. Resist him, steadfast in the faith, knowing that the same sufferings are experienced by your brotherhood in the world.*** **1Peter 5:8-9** It is up to me to choose to *overcome* the wiles of the devil and the worldly EGO spirit. In a *manifested Time Paradox*, God is allowing my brief *finite flesh* existence **James 4:14** to freely choose my *infinite spiritual* existence – to *stay with* or to *leave* my birthright family.

Preserved With A Believing Faith

Born again with an *inheritance* that can never perish, spoil or fade is a *birthright status*. In this section, I discuss maturing and keeping my focus on belief, faith and trust in Jesus in order to *avoid rejecting* my birthright inheritance. The following scriptures testify to the role of my belief, faith and action in *preserving* my birthright gift.

NKJV Scripture	NSECB Definitions

John 3:16-18. For God so loved the world that He gave His only begotten Son, that whoever believes[4100] in Him should not perish but have everlasting life. For God did not send His Son into the world[2889] to condemn[2919] the world[2889], but that the world[2889] through Him might be saved[4982]. He who believes[4100] in Him is not condemned[2919]; but he who does not believe is condemned[2919] already, because he has not believed[4100] in the name of the only begotten Son of God.

1John 1:8-10. If we say[2036] that we have no sin, we deceive ourselves, and the truth is not in us. If we confess[3670] our sins[0266], He is faithful and just to forgive[0863] us our sins and to cleanse[2511] us from all unrighteousness[0093]. If we say[2036] that we have not sinned, we make Him a liar, and His word is not in us.

1Cor 3:16-17. Do you not know that you are the temple of God and that the Spirit[4151] of God dwells[3611] in you? If anyone defiles the temple of God, God will destroy him. For the temple of God is holy, which temple you are.

Col 3:11. where there is neither Greek nor Jew, circumcised nor uncircumcised, barbarian, Scythian, slave nor free, but Christ is all[3956] and in all[3956].

Heb 8:10-12. For this is the covenant that I will make with the house of Israel after those days, says the LORD: **I will put My laws in their mind[1271] and write them on their hearts[2588]**; and I will be their God, and they shall be My people. **None of them shall teach his neighbor,** and none his brother, saying, 'Know the LORD,' **for all shall know Me, from the least of them to the greatest of them.** For I will be merciful to their unrighteousness, and their sins and their lawless deeds I will remember no more."

Rev 3:14-16. And to the angel of the church of the Laodiceans write, These things says the Amen, the Faithful and True Witness, the Beginning of the

[0093]**unrighteousness.** (legal) injustice (properly, the quality, by implication, the act); morally, wrongfulness (of character, life or act).

[0266]**sins.** a sin (properly abstract); to miss the mark, i.e., to err.

[0863]**forgive.** (to send; an intens. form of eimi, to go); to send forth.

[1271]**minds.** deep thought, properly, the faculty (mind or its disposition), by implication, its exercise.

[1692]**vomit.** of uncertain affinity; to vomit.

[2036]**say.** a primary verb (used only in the definite past tense, the others being borrowed from 2046, 4483, and 5346); to speak or say (by word or writing).

[2041]**works.** from a primary (but obsolete) ergo (to work); toil (as an effort or occupation); by implication, an act.

[2511]**cleanse.** to cleanse (literally or figuratively).

[2588]**hearts.** prolonged from a primary kar (Latin, cor, "heart"); the heart, i.e. (figuratively) the thoughts or feelings (mind); also (by analogy) the middle.

[2889]**world.** orderly arrangement, i.e. decoration; by implication, the world (in a wide or narrow sense, including its inhabitants, literally or figuratively [morally]).

[2919]**condemn.** properly, to distinguish, i.e. decide (mentally or judicially); by implication, to try, condemn, punish.

[3611]**dwells.** to occupy a house, i.e. reside (figuratively, inhabit, remain, inhere); by implication to cohabit.

[3670]**confess.** from a compound of the base of 3674 and 3056; to assent, i.e. covenant, acknowledge. THAYER = to admit or declare oneself guilty of what one is accused of: τὰς ἁμαρτίας, [1 John 1:9]

[3956]**all.** including all the forms of declension; apparently a primary word; all, any, every, the whole.

[4100]**believes.** to have faith (in, upon, or with respect to, a person or thing), i.e. credit; by implication, to entrust (especially one's spiritual well-being to Christ).

[4151]**Spirit.** a current of air, i.e. breath (blast) or a breeze; by analogy or figuratively, a spirit, i.e. (human) the rational soul, (by implication) vital principle, mental disposition, etc., or (superhuman) an angel, demon, or (divine) God, Christ's spirit, the

creation of God: "I know your works[2041], that you are neither cold nor hot. I could wish you were cold or hot. So then, because you are lukewarm, and neither cold nor hot, I will vomit[1692] you out of My mouth.

Holy Spirit.

[4982]saved. from a primary sos (contraction for obsolete saoz, "safe"); to save, i.e. deliver or protect (literally or figuratively).

Our careful and truthful reading of the preceding scriptures revealed to us the following uncomplicated precepts.

- God puts his laws directly into the minds and hearts of everyone.
  "I will put My laws in their mind and write them on their hearts... None of them shall teach his neighbor..." Heb 8:10

- God's Spirit resides in everyone.
  "Do you not know that you are the temple of God and that the Spirit of God dwells in you?" 1Cor 3:16

- *When I reach an age of understanding*, I must make a free will choice to not believe or believe in Jesus – reject or accept.
  "because you are lukewarm, and neither hot nor cold, I will vomit you out of my mouth" Rev 3:16

- Jesus comes to *all* who receive Him and believe in His name.
  "He came to His own, and His own did not receive Him. But as many as received Him, to them He gave the right to become children of God, to those who believe in His name" John 1:11-12

- Jesus gives to *all* the right to become children born of God – to be birthright heirs.
  "where there is neither Greek nor Jew, circumcised nor uncircumcised, barbarian, Scythian, slave nor free, but Christ is all and in all." Col 3:11

- *All* who believe in Jesus have eternal life.
  "...that whoever believes in Him should not perish but have everlasting life." John 3:16

- *All* who do not believe in Jesus stand condemned.
  "He who believes in Him is not condemned; but he who does not believe is condemned already, because he has not believed in the name of the only begotten Son of God." John 3:18

The emphasis is about *choices. When I reach an age of understanding*, if I *choose* to confess (*acknowledge and agree with Jesus*) that I sin by nature, Jesus will cast away my sins and cleanse me from all unrighteousness; if I *choose* to claim otherwise, the end result is not good. ***"If we say that we have no sin, we deceive ourselves, and the truth is not in us. If we confess our sins, He is faithful and just to forgive us our sins and to cleanse us from all unrighteousness. If we say that we have not sinned, we make Him a liar, and***

His word is not in us." [1John 1:8-10] The emphasis is not about my confessing sins, but rather, the emphasis is about my *choices.*

Free Will Choice – Flesh vs Spirit

> *"And the LORD God commanded the man, saying, 'Of every tree of the garden you may freely eat; but of the tree of the knowledge of good and evil you shall not eat, for in the day that you eat of it you shall surely die'."* [Gen 2:16-17] *... "So when the woman saw that the tree was good for food, that it was pleasant to the eyes, and a tree desirable to make one wise, she took of its fruit and ate. She also gave to her husband with her, and he ate."* [Gen 3:6]

Adam & Eve were created with a *flesh nature* and a *spiritual nature* – with the *free will to choose between the two.* Luke's account of the prodigal son parable is about *free will choices.* Likewise, as a descendent I was created with a *flesh nature* and a *spiritual nature* – with a *free will to choose.*

I inherited Adam's *flesh nature* – I did *not* inherit Adam's *original sin.* Inherited *flesh nature* does not equate to *imputed original sin.* Inherited *flesh nature* is the inherited EGO (**E**dge **G**od **O**ut) nature in me that has its own agenda apart from the Spirit of God residing in me. This distinction is communicated in Galatians.

> *"Do not be deceived, God is not mocked; for whatever a man sows, that he will also reap. For he who sows to his flesh will of the flesh reap corruption, but he who sows to the Spirit will of the Spirit reap everlasting life.* [Gal 6:7-8]
>
> *Note.* Some versions translate *sinful nature* and *nature* in lieu of *flesh.* These are more subjective interpretation than objective translation. The Greek equivalent reads *flesh*, which preserves the Greek contrast between *flesh* vs *spirit.*

I have a free will that can choose the guidance of the *infinite* Holy Spirit in me or choose the agenda of the *finite* flesh nature in me (sometimes a/k/a sin nature). This choice is communicated in Romans and Luke.

> *"For if you live according to the flesh you will die; but if by the Spirit you put to death the deeds of the body, you will live. For as many as are led by the Spirit of God, these are sons of God."* [Rom 8:13-14]

> *"But Jesus called them to Him and said, 'Let the little children come to Me, and do not forbid them; for of such is the kingdom of God. Assuredly, I say to you, whoever does not receive the kingdom of God as a little child will by no means enter it'."* [Luke 18:16-17]

The message – A little child puts his belief and trust in earthly parents. I likewise, as a child of God, must *choose, believe and trust* the guidance of the Holy Spirit residing in me.

Lasse-faire indifference won't cut it. Jesus warns the Laodiceans about the pretend languid comfort of a middle of the road attitude.

> *"So then, because you are lukewarm, and neither cold nor hot,*
> *I will vomit you out of My mouth."* *Rev 3:16*

The message – most of us reach that age of understanding where we must make that *free will* choice. I must either (i) defect and join the world blaspheming the Holy Spirit, denying Jesus and rejecting salvation, or (ii) confess (*acknowledge and agree with*) Jesus and live in my *family inheritance*.

In our *flesh time*, *I AM* gives each of us a free will spirit where I am either rejecting Jesus and following the proud EGO of the world or I am a trusting child of God accepting Jesus as my lord and savior. Jesus explains.

> *"and said, 'Assuredly, I say to you, unless you are converted and*
> *become as little children, you will by no means enter the kingdom*
> *of heaven.'"* *Matt 18:3*

The message – eternal life is mission impossible without an all-encompassing belief and trust in Jesus. My flesh's proud bragging EGO must be *surrendered*.

Both God and Jesus declared *I AM* – not I WAS – not I WILL BE. Similarly, God and Jesus *fulfill* their part of the new covenant – not was fulfilled – not will be fulfilled.

> *"For we who have believed do enter that rest, as He has said:*
> *'So I swore in My wrath, They shall not enter My rest,'*
> *although the works were finished from the foundation*
> *[creation] of the world."* *Heb 4:3*

The message – the *I AM* Jesus fulfilled the covenant from the foundation [creation] of the world. It's up to me to make my free will choice – death vs eternal life.

Eternal Life vs Death

While contemplating the promise of eternal life to *"he who overcomes"* the world, I found myself contemplating the true meaning, vastness and timelessness of the *infinite* eternal life concept – a concept that is too often expediently minimized and glossed over. The following scriptures give us a realistic preview into the *good, the bad and the ugly* of eternal eternity – it is my choice.

NKJV Scripture	NSECB Definitions
John 3:14-16. And as Moses lifted up the serpent in the wilderness, even **so must the Son of Man be lifted up, that whoever believes in Him should not perish but have eternal[0166] life[2222]**. For God so loved the world that He gave His only begotten Son, that **whoever believes in Him should not perish[0622] but have everlasting[0166] life[2222]**.	[0086]**hades.** properly, unseen, i.e. "Hades" or the place (state) of departed souls. [0166]**everlasting, eternal.** perpetual (also used of past time, or past and future as well). [0191]**hears.** a primary verb; to hear (in various senses). [0622]**perish.** to destroy fully (reflexively, to perish, or lose), literally or figuratively. [0931]**torment.** a touch-stone, i.e. (by analogy) torture. [1208]**second.** (ordinal) second (in time, place, or rank; also adverb).
John 5:22-24. For the Father judges no one, but has committed all judgment to the Son, that all should honor the Son just as they honor the Father. He who does not honor the Son does not honor the Father who sent Him. "Most assuredly, I say to you, **he who hears[0191] My word[3056] and believes[4100] in Him who sent Me has everlasting[0166] life[2222], and shall not come into judgment, but has passed from death[2288] into life[2222]**.	[2222]**life.** life (literally or figuratively). [2288]**death.** (properly, an adjective used as a noun) death (literally or figuratively). [2545]**burns.** apparently a primary verb; to set on fire, i.e. kindle or (by implication) consume. [2816]**inherit.** to be an heir to (literally or figuratively). [3041]**lake.** (through the idea of nearness of shore); a pond (large or small).
Luke 16:22-25. So it was that the beggar died, and was carried by the angels to Abraham's bosom. The rich man also died and was buried. **And being in torments[0931] in Hades[0086]**, he lifted up his eyes and saw Abraham afar off, and Lazarus in his bosom. Then he cried and said, Father Abraham, have mercy on me, and send Lazarus that he may dip the tip of his finger in water and cool my tongue; for I am tormented in this flame. But Abraham said, Son, remember that in your lifetime you received your good things, and likewise Lazarus evil things; but **now he is comforted[3870] and you are tormented[3600]**.	[3056]**word.** something said (including the thought); by implication a topic (subject of discourse), also reasoning (the mental faculty) or motive; by extension, a computation; specifically (with the article in John) the Divine Expression (i.e. Christ). [3600]**tormented.** to grieve. [3709]**wrath.** properly, desire (as a reaching forth or excitement of the mind), i.e. (by analogy,) violent passion (ire, or [justifiable] abhorrence); by implication punishment.
Rev 21:6-8. And He said to me, It is done! I am the Alpha and the Omega, the Beginning and the End. **I will give of the fountain of the water[5204] of life[2222] freely to him who thirsts. He who overcomes shall inherit[2816] all things, and I will be his God and he shall be My son. But the cowardly, unbelieving, abominable, murderers, sexually immoral, sorcerers, idolaters, and all liars shall have their part in the lake[3041] which burns[2545] with fire[4442] and brimstone, which is the second[1208] death[2288]**.	[3870]**comforted.** to call near, i.e. invite, invoke (by imploration, hortation or consolation). [4100]**believes.** to have faith (in, upon, or with respect to, a person or thing), i.e. credit; by implication, to entrust (especially one's spiritual well-being to Christ). [4442]**fire.** a primary word; "fire" (literally or figuratively, specifically, lightning). [5204]**water.** water (as if rainy) literally or figuratively.
John 3:35-36. The Father loves the Son, and has given all things into His hand. **He who believes[4100] in the Son has everlasting[0166] life[2222]; and he who does not believe the Son shall not see life, but the wrath[3709] of God abides on him**."	
Rom 6:23. For the wages of sin is death[2288], but the gift of God is eternal[0166] life[2222] in Christ Jesus our Lord.	

The bottom line – my choices for my very, very, very long eternity include:

- **death vs life** *John 5:22-24*
- **torment vs comforted** *Luke 16:22-25*
- **lake which burns with fire vs water of life** *Rev 21:6-8*
- **wrath of God's vs everlasting life** *John 3:35-36*
- **death vs life** *Rom 6:23*

It is my free will choice – my eternity choice is *"either/or"* – there is no oblivious agnostic middle ground. The story of Lazarus and the rich man is clear – *either* eternal torment *or* eternal comfort. *Luke 16:22-25*.

Blasphemy Against The Holy Spirit

The emphasis for me is not about *obtaining* my salvation, but rather, it is about *not rejecting* God's gift. Blasphemy against the Holy Spirit *residing in me* is the *unforgiveable sin* – it is *rejecting* God's gift.   In order to fully understand Blasphemy Against The Holy Spirit, we must first understand the meaning of blasphemy, grieving and kingdom.

- *Blasphemy* is from the Greek *blasphemia,* which refers to debasing, derogatory, nasty, shameful, ugly speech or behavior that is intended to humiliate someone else.   Paul used the word blasphemer to describe his own past words and actions against the new Christians. Blasphemy against the Holy Spirit is a continual and obstinate rejection of the truth of the Word and a denial of the truth and guidance of the Holy Spirit. Blasphemy against the Holy Spirit grieves the Holy Spirit that resides in me, which in turn causes me to be a *spiritual house divided.*
- *Grieving* is from the Greek word *lupete,* which is from the word *lupe,* which denotes a *pain* or *grief* that can only be experienced between two people who deeply love each other. This word *lupe* would normally be used to picture a husband or wife who has discovered his or her mate has been unfaithful. As a result of this choice to be unfaithful, the betrayed spouse feels the pain that accompanies unfaithfulness. The Holy Spirit longs for us, thinks about us, desires to be close to us, and wants to reveal Himself to us. However, when we choose to act like the world, choose to talk like the world, choose to behave like the world, and choose to respond the same way the world does, we cause the Spirit of God to feel shock, hurt, and grief. When we deliberately choose to do what is wrong, we drag the Holy Spirit into the mire of sin with us, because He lives in us and goes wherever we go.
- *Kingdom* is from the Greek word *basileuoo,* which refers to the territory subject to the rule of a king.   The domain of a king is the territory over which he exercises authority, control, and dominion. A king is the legal owner of all that is in his domain (*that includes you and me*).   Another word for owner is lord – a king is automatically lord. When the king impacts the domain with his influence it is called his *kingdom.*

If I choose to blaspheme and grieve the Holy Spirit and to seek the guidance of the world, I will have made a deadly choice (i) to put my worldly EGO in charge, (ii) to reject God's gift of Jesus as my Lord and savior, and (iii) to be a *house divided against the Holy Spirit* that resides in me.

45

*Blasphemy is all about the heart and spirit of the blasphemer.
If I were the Holy Spirit of God, would I want to reside in me?*

The scriptures testify to the character and personality of God's *kingdom* plan and the tragic destiny for anyone who still chooses to be a *blasphemous house divided*.

NKJV Scripture	LaForge Commentary
Luke 11:9-13. So I say to you, ask, and it will be given to you; seek, and you will find; knock, and it will be opened to you. For everyone who asks receives, and he who seeks finds, and to him who knocks it will be opened... how much more will your heavenly Father give the Holy Spirit to those who ask Him!	*Commentary*: The Word very clearly instructs me to ask for and seek the guidance of the Holy Spirit.
Luke 11:17. But He, knowing their thoughts, said to them: Every kingdom divided against itself is brought to desolation, and a house divided against a house falls. **Luke 12:10.** And anyone who speaks a word against the Son of Man, it will be forgiven him; but to him who blasphemes against the Holy Spirit, it will not be forgiven. **Luke 17:20-21.** ...He answered them and said, The kingdom of God does not come with observation; nor will they say, See here! or See there! For indeed, **the kingdom of God is within you.**"	*Commentary*: A blasphemer becomes a house divided against himself – a dissenter in the kingdom. In Jesus' eternal life kingdom, there cannot be any dissenters – it is just that simple. There cannot be any dissenters **because the kingdom of God is within each of us.**
Mark 3:23-26. ...How can Satan cast out Satan? If a kingdom is divided against itself, that kingdom cannot stand. And if a house is divided against itself, that house cannot stand. And if Satan has risen up against himself, and is divided, he cannot stand, but has an end.	*Commentary*: Dissenters are idolaters with an EGO spirit in opposition to the Holy Spirit – they simply will not be allowed to enter into and create strife in Jesus' eternal life kingdom.
Gal 5:16-17. I say then: Walk in the Spirit, and you shall not fulfill the lust of the flesh. **For the flesh lusts against the Spirit, and the Spirit against the flesh; and these are contrary to one another**, so that you do not do the things that you wish.	*Commentary*: Those who follow their finite flesh desires are following desires contrary to the Holy Spirit in them – i.e., would be dissenters and disrupters in Jesus' eternal life kingdom.

Jesus' eternal life kingdom is a *spirit* filled life. I must choose to reject the worldly norm of succumbing to my *finite* flesh desires and to instead remain with the spiritual guidance of the *infinite* Holy Spirit. *Jesus is looking at my heart and spirit – at me believing in Jesus as savior and Lord and having faith in his promise.* In our manifested earthly life, Jesus is blotting out the defectors, insurgents and the EGO proud – those that would divide and cause strife in the eternal life kingdom.

Blasphemy appears in both Old and New Testament times. In the old covenant, God spoke to his people through Moses and the prophets – some chose to blaspheme God by refusing to follow the guidance of the patriarchs. In the new covenant, God speaks to his people directly through the Holy Spirit – some choose to blaspheme the Holy Spirit by refusing to follow the guidance of the Holy Spirit. The following scriptures continue with God's take on the matter of blasphemy.

NKJV Scripture	NSECB Definitions
1Tim 1:13-14. **although I was formerly a blasphemer[0989], a persecutor, and an insolent man; but I obtained mercy because I did it ignorantly in unbelief.** And the grace of our Lord was exceedingly abundant, with faith and love which are in Christ Jesus.	[0166]**eternal.** perpetual (also used of past time, or past and future as well). [0265]**sins, condemnation.** a sin (properly concrete). [0629]**redemption.** (the act) ransom in full, i.e. (figuratively) riddance, or (specially) Christian salvation. [0987]**blasphemes.** to vilify; specially, to speak impiously. [0988]**blasphemy.** vilification (especially against God). [0989]**blasphemer.** from a derivative of **984** and **5345**; scurrilious, i.e. calumnious (against men), or (specially) impious (against God). Blasphemos. **984** a primary verb; properly, to hinder, i.e. (by implication) to injure. **5345** from 5346; a saying, i.e. rumor. **5346** the same as the base of 5457 and 5316; to show or make known one's thoughts, i.e. speak or say. [3076]**grieve.** to distress; reflexively or passively, to be sad. [4972]**you were sealed.** to stamp (with a signet or private mark) for security or preservation (literally or figuratively); by implication, to keep secret, to attest.
Matt 12:30-32. **He who is not with Me is against Me**, and he who does not gather with Me scatters abroad. Therefore I say to you, **every sin and blasphemy[0988] will be forgiven men, but the blasphemy[0988] against the Spirit will not be forgiven men.** Anyone who speaks a word against the Son of Man, it will be forgiven him; but **whoever speaks against the Holy Spirit, it will not be forgiven him, either in this age or in the age to come.**	
Mark 3:28-29. Assuredly, I say to you, all sins[0265] will be forgiven the sons of men, and whatever blasphemies[0987] they may utter; **but he who blaspheme[0987] against the Holy Spirit never has forgiveness, but is subject to eternal[0166] condemnation[0265].**	
Eph 4:30-5:5. And **do not grieve[3076] the Holy Spirit of God, by whom you were sealed[4972] for the day of redemption[0629]. Let all bitterness, wrath, anger, clamor, and evil speaking be put away from you, with all malice. And be kind to one another, tenderhearted, forgiving one another, even as God in Christ forgave you.** Therefore be imitators of God as dear children. And walk in love, as Christ also has loved us and given Himself for us, an offering and a sacrifice to God for a sweet-smelling aroma. But fornication and all uncleanness or covetousness, let it not even be named among you, as is fitting for saints; neither filthiness, nor foolish talking, nor coarse jesting, which are not fitting, but rather giving of thanks. **For this you know, that no fornicator, unclean person, nor covetous man, who is an idolater, has any inheritance in the kingdom of Christ and God.**	

In Paul's letter to Timothy, Paul acknowledges that he was once a *blasphemer* and a persecutor and a violent man, but was shown mercy *because he was acting in ignorance and unbelief.* It is significant that Paul was forgiven his *blasphemy* after he repented from his *blasphemous* beliefs and in turn became a believing champion for Jesus. Paul changed his belief system in light of learning the truth. Since *blaspheming* the Holy Spirit is a deadly serious matter, I am including a study of Galatians. Galatians 5:19 plainly lists *finite* flesh desires that can steer me to a life that is *blasphemy* to the Holy Spirit *residing in me.* The Word plainly warns me that if these flesh cravings overtake and control my life, I will **"not inherit the kingdom of God"** *Gal 5:21*. The Word plainly reads **"For he who sows to his flesh will of the flesh reap corruption, but he who sows to the Spirit will of the Spirit reap everlasting life."** *Gal 6:8*.

Each of the Holy Spirit's chosen words in Galatians 5:19-21 are pungent and powerful – important to the Holy Spirit – therefore, important to me. The Holy Spirit *residing in me* wants me to be able to identify and prohibit these works of the flesh in my life. I looked deep into the Greek meaning and context of each listed manifestation of the flesh. It is of utmost importance that I understand exactly what God's Word is saying. The works of the flesh can blindly and devastatingly steer me into a *hardened heart* – steer me *away from* following the Holy Spirit – steer me to the alternative of *blaspheming* the Holy Spirit and becoming a *house divided* and *rejecting* eternal life.

Galatians 5:19-21 reads as follows. *"Now the works of the flesh[4561] are evident, which are: adultery[9999], fornication[4202], uncleanness[0167], lewdness[0766], idolatry[1495], sorcery[5331], hatred[2189], contentions[2054], jealousies[2205], outbursts of wrath[2372], selfish ambitions[2052], dissensions[1370], heresies[0139], envy[5355], murders[9999], drunkenness[3178], revelries[2970], and the like; of which I tell you beforehand, just as I also told you in time past, that those who practice such things will not inherit the kingdom of God."*

Appendix B is a detailed discussion of each *act of the flesh[4561]*. The Greek to English translations are quite misleading in many instances. In many instances, the underlying Greek word will shock and surprise the often malformed perception inferred by its English translation counterpart. It is extremely important that each of us study and fully comprehend the full scope of each listed act.

The preceding list in Galatians encompasses a broad spectrum of desires and works driven by the *finite* carnal flesh – our *inherited flesh nature*. A sinful act out of human weakness is one thing – I am cleansed by the blood. A habitual lifestyle choice to *consciously reject* the guidance of the Holy Spirit *in me* is another – it is both thought and action *blaspheming* the Holy Spirit *residing in me*. As James warns us, *I must look to God, not to man*.

NKJV Scripture	NSECB Definitions
James 1:14-15. But each one is tempted when he is drawn away by his own desires[1939] and enticed. Then, when desire has conceived, it gives birth to sin; and sin, when it is full-grown[0658], brings forth death.	[0658]**full-grown.** to complete entirely, i.e. consummate. [1939]**desire.** a longing (especially for what is forbidden).

Am I deceiving myself and conjoining with blasphemy? When I abandon God's truths in favor of *consensus morality*, I am rejecting the guidance of the Holy Spirit. When I engage in *consensus depravity*, I drag the Holy Spirit through the mire of my sin. When I *renounce God's creation order*, I am undermining God's plan. At some point, continually running alongside blasphemy can harden anyone's heart and give birth to death. As Jesus warns us, if this is me, I must transform my thinking now and turn to the voice of the Holy Spirit.

NKJV Scripture	NSECB Definitions
Matt 10:28. And do not fear those who kill the body but cannot kill the soul. But rather fear Him who is able to destroy both soul and body in hell[1067].	[1067]**hell.** of Hebrew origin [OT:1516 and OT:2011]; valley of (the son of) Hinnom; ge-henna (or Ge-Hinnom), a valley of Jerusalem, used (figuratively) as a name for the place (or state) of everlasting punishment.

Jesus is *blotting out of His book of life* anyone who makes a free will choice to abandon the guidance of the *infinite* Holy Spirit and instead succumb totally to the self-interest desires of the *finite* flesh. A valuable reality check is to ask ourselves "If I were Jesus *blotting out* the dissenters, disrupters and rule-breakers from my *book of life* for my shared *infinite* eternal life family, would I say I never knew me or would I keep me?"

To He Who Overcomes

The Word is clear about the dreadfully horrific wrath if I willfully and perversely reject Jesus and submit to my carnal flesh desires. The Word is equally clear about the incredibly good gift for me if I believe and have faith in Jesus and persevere to crucify my carnal EGO flesh desires.

The Word instructs us ***"I beseech you therefore, brethren, by the mercies of God, that you present your bodies a living sacrifice, holy, acceptable to God, which is your reasonable service.*** *Rom 12:1*. In the old covenant, an animal sacrifice could only be presented only once because the animal was dead. In the new covenant, I am instructed to offer myself as a *"living sacrifice"*; i.e., I must commit to live in a continual state of *surrender* to Jesus. For some, the commitment may arise with a momentous decision from the depths of insurrection *(that momentous aha moment)*; for others the commitment may be a gradual growing fulfillment *(no unique aha moment)*. In either event, my total commitment must be sustained with my daily decision to *surrender* myself to Jesus as my Lord. Each day I must renew my commitment – yesterday is yesterday's sphere. My *finite carnal nature* will likely declare war on my decisions to *surrender* completely to Jesus as my Lord, so I must be prepared to do battle. The following scriptures speak directly to *surrendering* to Jesus.

NKJV Scripture	NSECB Definitions
John 3:35-36. The Father loves the Son, and has given all things into His hand. **He who believes[4100] in the Son has everlasting life; and he who does not believe[0544] the Son shall not see life, but the wrath of God abides on him.**	[0166]**eternal.** perpetual (also used of past time, or past and future as well). [0225]**truth.** truth. [0544]**not believe.** to disbelieve (wilfully and perversely). [0571]**unbelieving.** disbelieving, i.e. without Christian faith (specially, a heathen); (passively) untrustworthy (person), or incredible (thing). [0726]**snatch.** to sieze (in various applications). [0948]**vile.** from a (presumed) derivative of bdeo (to stink); to be disgusted, i.e. (by implication) detest (especially of idolatry). [1169]**cowardly.** from deos (dread); timid, i.e. (by implication) faithless. [1496]**idolators.** an image- servant or) worshipper (literally or figuratively). [2222]**life.** life (literally or figuratively). [3528]**overcomes.** to subdue (literally or figuratively). [4100]**believes.** to have faith (in, upon, or with respect to, a person or thing), i.e. credit; by implication, to entrust (especially one's spiritual well-being to Christ).
John 4:23. But the hour is coming, and now is, when the **true worshipers will worship[4352] the Father in spirit[4151] and truth[0225]**; for the Father is seeking such to worship Him.	
John 10:27-30. My sheep hear My voice, and I know them, and they follow Me. And **I give them eternal[0166] life[2222], and they shall never perish; neither shall anyone snatch[0726] them out of My hand[5495]. My Father, who has given them to Me, is greater than all; and no one is able to**	

snatch[0726] them out of My Father's hand[5495]. I and My Father are one.

LaForge Commentary. No one can *"snatch"* me from my Fathers' hand; but I can make a fatal choice to *reject* Jesus.

Rev 21:6-8. And He said to me, It is done! I am the Alpha and the Omega, the Beginning and the End. I will give of the fountain of the water of life freely to him who thirsts. **He who overcomes[3528] shall inherit all things, and I will be his God and he shall be My son. But the cowardly[1169], unbelieving[0571], abominable[0948], murderers[5406], sexually immoral[4205], sorcerers[5332], idolaters[1496], and all liars[5571] shall have their part in the lake which burns with fire and brimstone, which is the second death.**

[4151]**Spirit.** a current of air, i.e. breath (blast) or a breeze; by analogy or figuratively, a spirit, i.e. (human) the rational soul, (by implication) vital principle, mental disposition, etc., or (superhuman) an angel, demon, or (divine) God, Christ's spirit, the Holy Spirit.

[4205]**sexually immoral.** from pernemi (to sell; akin to the base of 4097); a (male) prostitute (as venal), i.e. (by analogy) a debauchee (libertine).

[4352]**worship.** (meaning to kiss, like a dog licking his master's hand); to fawn or crouch to, i.e. (literally or figuratively) prostrate oneself in homage (do reverence to, adore).

[5332]**practice magic arts.** from pharmakon (a drug, i.e. spell-giving potion); a druggist ("pharmacist") or poisoner, i.e. (by extension) a magician.

[5406]**murderers.** to be a murderer (of).

[5495]**hand.** the hand (literally or figuratively [power]; especially [by Hebraism] a means or instrument).

[5571]**liars.** untrue, i.e. erroneous, deceitful, wicked.

Jesus' sacrificial death for my sins against mankind renders me righteous before God – it is a birthright gift. Jesus' resurrection gives me a born again status into the inheritance of eternal life – it is a birthright gift. Jesus has given me authority to overcome the power of the world's spirit. For my part, overcoming the world spirit and "keeping" the birthright gift of eternal life is all about my *overcoming* the temptations of carnal fleshly desires. The following scriptures speak directly to *overcoming*.

NKJV Scripture	NSECB Definitions
2Pet 2:20. For if, after they have escaped[0668] the pollutions of the world through the knowledge[1922] of the Lord and Savior Jesus Christ, they are again[3825] entangled[1707] in them and overcome[2274], the latter end is worse for them than the beginning[4413].	[0668]**escaped.** (figuratively) to escape.
	[0926]**burdensome.** weighty, i.e. (fig) burdensome, grave.
1John 5:1-5. Whoever believes that Jesus is the Christ is born of God, and everyone who loves Him who begot also loves him who is begotten of Him. By this we know that we love the children of God, when we love God and keep His commandments. For this is the love of God, that we keep His commandments. **And His commandments are not burdensome[0926]. For whatever[3956-3588] is born[1080] of God overcomes[3528] the world. And this is the victory that has overcome[3528] the world — our faith. Who is he who overcomes[3528] the world, but he who believes[4100] that Jesus is the Son of God?**	[1080]**born.** to procreate (properly, of the father, but by extension of the mother); figuratively, to regenerate
	[1707]**entangled.** to entwine, i.e. (figuratively) involve with.
	[1922]**knowledge.** recognition, i.e. (by implication) full discernment, acknowledgement.
	[2274]**overcome.** to make worse, i.e. vanquish (literally or figuratively); by implication, to rate lower.
	[3528]**overcomes.** to subdue (literally or figuratively).
Rev 2:7. He who has an ear, let him hear what the Spirit says to the churches. **To him who overcomes[3528] I will give to eat from the tree of life, which is in the midst of the Paradise of God.**	[3825]**again.** probably from the same as 3823 (through the idea of oscillatory repetition); (adverbially) anew, i.e. (of place) back, (of time) once more, or (conjunctionally) furthermore or on the other hand.
Rev 2:10-11. Do not fear any of those things which you are about to suffer. Indeed, the devil is about to throw some of you into prison, that you may be tested, and you will have tribulation ten days. Be faithful until death, and I will give you the crown of life. He who	[3528]**overcomes.** to subdue (literally or figuratively).
	[3956-3588]**whatever.** [3956] including all the forms of declension; apparently

has an ear, let him hear what the Spirit says to the churches. **He who overcomes[3528] shall not be hurt by the second death.**

Rev 2:17. ...To him who overcomes[3528] I will give some of the hidden manna to eat. And I will give him a white stone, and on the stone a new name written which no one knows except him who receives it.

Rev 2:26. And he who overcomes[3528], and keeps My works until the end, to him I will give power over the nations...

Rev 3:5. He who overcomes[3528] shall be clothed in white garments, and I will not blot out his name from the Book of Life; but I will confess his name before My Father and before His angels.

Rev 3:11-12. Behold, I am coming quickly! Hold fast what you have, that no one may take your crown. **He who overcomes[3528], I will make him a pillar in the temple of My God, and he shall go out no more.** I will write on him the name of My God and the name of the city of My God, the New Jerusalem, which comes down out of heaven from My God. And I will write on him My new name.

James 1:12. Blessed is the man who endures[5278] temptation[3986]; for when he has been approved, he will receive the crown of life which the Lord has promised to those who love Him.

a primary word; all, any, every, the whole. [3588] ho (ho); including the feminine he (hay); and the neuter to (to); in all their inflections.
[3986]temptation. a putting to proof (by experiment [of good], experience [of evil], solicitation, discipline or provocation); by implication, adversity.
[4100]believes. to have faith (in, upon, or with respect to, a person or thing), i.e. credit; by implication, to entrust (especially one's spiritual well-being to Christ).
[4413]beginning. foremost (in time, place, order or importance).
[5278]endures. to stay under (behind), i.e. remain; figuratively, to undergo, i.e. bear (trials), have fortitude, persevere.

It's not about what I can do or the works I can perform to attain righteous status and inherit eternal life. It's all about me *overcoming* to preserve my birthright inheritance of eternal life with Jesus.

Retaining my birthright salvation is *overcoming the spirit of the world* and *not blaspheming the Holy Spirit residing in me*. Once I reach the age of understanding, I must make the clear, affirmative and definitive free will choice to listen to the Holy Spirit, follow Jesus and overcome the world. As for lukewarm, Jesus gives his take when he says:

Rev 3:14 *"And to the angel of the church of the Laodiceans write, These things says the Amen, the Faithful and True Witness, the Beginning of the creation of God: I know your works, that you are neither cold nor hot. I could wish you were cold or hot. So then, because you are lukewarm, and neither cold nor hot, I will vomit you out of My mouth. Because you say, I am rich, have become wealthy, and have need of nothing' — and do not know that you are wretched, miserable, poor, blind, and naked — "*

Laodicea was the biggest and richest city in the local area, but it had neither hot nor cold water. Nearby Colosse had cold waters; nearby Hierapolis had hot springs. Laodiceans had to leave their comfort zone to enjoy either hot or cold waters. Instead of going to the water, Laodicea tried to pipe in hot water from Hierapolis, but the water arrived lukewarm with a sickening, nauseating taste. In the same way, Laodiceans were lukewarm in their beliefs towards Jesus – neither cool and refreshing nor hot and healing – stuck in the middle and nauseatingly distasteful to Jesus. Hence Jesus' statement *"vomit you out of my mouth"*.

An agnostic or middle of the road Laodicean attitude in worldly comforts just won't cut it. I cannot play dumb or plead ignorance or take the middle of the road or be a friend to the entire world or etc., etc. Most of us eventually reach the age of *understanding* where we must make that *free will choice* to either (i) be part of the world denying Jesus, or (ii) confess [agree with] Jesus as my Lord and Savior.

Jesus summarizes it all for us and gives us his take when he says:

Rev 21:6   *"**And He said to me,** It is done! I am the Alpha and the Omega, the Beginning and the End. I will give of the fountain of the water of life freely to him who thirsts. He who overcomes shall inherit all things, and I will be his God and he shall be My son. But the cowardly, unbelieving, abominable, murderers, sexually immoral, sorcerers, idolaters, and all liars shall have their part in the lake which burns with fire and brimstone, which is the second death."*

Mat 7:21   *"Not everyone who says to Me, Lord, Lord, shall enter the kingdom of heaven, but he who does the will of My Father in heaven."*

As for me, I choose to *overcome* the world and *retain* my birthright inheritance of eternal life with Jesus.

———— ♦ ————

Epilog

Throughout God's written Word, we discovered a predominant overriding theme. I am learning to embrace the following truths.

- Both God and Jesus refer to themselves as *"I AM"*.

- There is a Time Paradox *manifesting* both *God's infinity* and *man's finite flesh*. Jesus both is and was with God at the beginning of creation. All things were created by, through and for Jesus. Jesus is Lord of and over all of His kingdom.

- Jesus' victory over Satan occurred before *man's finite flesh time* began. Jesus' human birth in Bethlehem was not His beginning but merely *His manifestation to man* – a brief appearance in His eternal existence. Jesus is revealed in these last times for our sake. Jesus' work has been finished since before the creation of the world.

- The new covenant is God's promise of forgiveness to each of us.

- The new covenant is God's promise, through the Holy Spirit in each of us, to speak directly to the minds and hearts of each of us.

- Jesus offered himself as a ransom for *all mankind* (no one is excluded). Jesus offered himself to *cleanse* my conscience from acts that lead to death. Jesus is the mediator of the new covenant promise from God to me. Jesus, as the final sacrifice, is the only way to the Father and to eternal life.

- God, Moses, David, Paul, John and Jesus acknowledge that names are written in the *Lamb's Book of Life* unless *blotted out*.

- The eternal life gift for me is in Jesus and Jesus only. It is through Jesus' *sacrifice* that I am *born righteous* before God – it is a *birthright gift*. It is through Jesus' *resurrection* that I am *born again* – it is a *birthright gift*. I am born a child/son/heir of God into the *eternal life* kingdom by the *gift* of God's grace.

- Childhood innocence expires with the age of understanding. As each of us reaches the age of *understanding*, we must mature by refocusing our belief, faith and trust from our earthly parents to full belief, faith and trust in Jesus. I must make my *free will choice* to either (i) defect and join the *finite* world blaspheming the Holy Spirit and *rejecting* salvation, or (ii) confess *[agree with]* Jesus and live in my *family inheritance*.

- I must make my *free will choice* to: (i) *believe* in my heart Jesus is my Lord and savior (ii) *accept* Jesus as my Lord and savior, (iii) *have faith* in Jesus as my Lord and savior, and (iv) *trust* in Jesus as my Lord and savior. Like an innocent child, I must put my full belief, acceptance, faith and trust in Jesus.

- No amount of works, altar calls, deeds or good intentions can earn or obtain *born again* status for any of us.

- *Submission* with love is a sign of strength, not weakness. The central theme of Jesus' manifestation on earth was *submission* to the will of His Father.

- *Blasphemy* is the opposite of *submission.*

- *Blasphemy* against the Holy Spirit *that resides in me* leads to death and the loss of my eternal life gift. Jesus has given me authority over the power of the worldly desires. If I deliberately keep on sinning after knowing the truth, I am (i) *blaspheming* the Holy Spirit, (ii) *hardening* my heart, (iii) *becoming* a house divided, and (iv) *rejecting* my inheritance.

- Eternal life is the promise to *"those who overcome"* the *finite* world and *retain* their birthright *infinite* inheritance. For my part, *keeping* my pure grace birthright gift of eternal life is all about my *overcoming* my *inherited flesh nature [in some versions a/k/a sin nature]* and making a *free will choice* to follow the guidance of the Holy Spirit that resides in me – that voice inside me from God.

God's Word teaches **a** *child/son/heir of God relationship...*

It is *not* about doing stuff to become a part of God's family. Everyone is conceived in the womb as a *born again child/son/heir of God* with all the benefits of family eternal life inheritance.

It *is* about *overcoming* the prodigal temptations of the world. I must *submit to* (*not blaspheme*) the guidance of the Holy Spirit residing inside me and *preserve* (*not reject*) my birthright eternal life inheritance.

It *is* my *life vs death choice – blasphemy against the Holy Spirit residing inside me makes me a spiritual house divided – such blasphemy is the unforgiveable sin –* I must refute and *overcome* the worldly deceptions and enticements. I belong to Jesus – Jesus is my savior – Jesus is my Lord – Jesus is my Master.

...a relationship in my heart – in my inner being.

For The Bible Tells Me So

PART III

Appendices

Appendix A

This Appendix A List of Denominations is a summary listing taken from *Handbook of Denominations in the United States, 11ᵗʰ Edition.* Copyright© 1985, 4990, 1995, 2001 by Abingdon Press. Used by permission of Abingdon Press.

—————♦—————

List of Denominations

In the United States there are approximately 200 diverse denominational organizations that label themselves a church. A detailed discussion of each of the following listed organizations is presented in the 397 page *Handbook of Denominations in the United States, 11ᵗʰ Edition.*

Adventist Churches

Advent Christian Church ♦ Branch Davidians ♦ Church of God General Conference ♦ Church of God (Seventh Day) ♦ Seventh-day Adventist

Baha'i

Baptist Churches

Alliance of Baptist Churches ♦ American Baptist Association ♦ American Baptist Churches in the U.S.A. ♦ Baptist General Conference ♦ Cooperative Baptist Fellowship ♦ General Association of General Baptist Churches ♦ General Association of Regular Baptist Churches ♦ National Association of Free Will Baptists ♦ National Baptist Convention of America, Inc ♦ National Baptist Convention, U.S.A., Inc. ♦ National Missionary Baptist Convention of America ♦ National Primitive Baptist Convention, U.S.A. ♦ North American Baptist Conference ♦ Primitive Baptist ♦ Progressive National Baptist Convention, Inc ♦ Reformed or Sovereign Grace Baptists ♦ Separate Baptists in Christ (General Association) ♦ Seventh Day Baptist General Conference ♦ Southern Baptist Convention

Brethren and Pietist Churches

Brethren Church (Ashland) ♦ Brethren in Christ Church ♦ Church of God (Anderson, Indiana) ♦ Church of the Brethren ♦ Church of the United Brethren in Christ ♦ Evangelical Covenant Church ♦ Evangelical Free Church of America ♦ Fellowship of Grace Brethren Churches ♦ Moravian Church *(Unitas Fratrum)* ♦ Old German Baptist Brethren (Old Order Dunkers) ♦ Unity of the Brethren

Catholic Churches

American Catholic Church ♦ Eastern Rite Catholic/Uniate Churches ♦ Liberal Catholic Church ♦ Mariavite Old Catholic Church, Province of North America ♦ Old Catholic Churches ♦ Polish National Catholic Church of America ♦ Roman Catholic Church

Christian Churches (The Stone-Campbell Movement)
Christadelphians ♦ Christian Church (Disciples of Christ) ♦ Christian Churches and Churches of Christ ♦ Christian Congregation, Inc. ♦ Churches of Christ ♦ Church of Christ, Scientist (Christian Science) ♦ Church of God and Saints of Christ ♦ Community Churches, International Council of

Congregational Churches
Congregational Christian Churches (National Association) ♦ Conservative Congregational Christian Conference ♦ United Church of Christ ♦ Divine Science

Episcopal/Anglican Churches
Anglican Catholic Church ♦ Episcopal Church ♦ Episcopal Orthodox Christian Archdiocese of America ♦ International Communion of the Charismatic Episcopal Church ♦ National Organization of the New Apostolic Church of North America ♦ Reformed Episcopal Church ♦ Southern Episcopal Church

Friends (Quaker)
Evangelical Friends International ♦ Friends General Conference ♦ Friends United Meeting ♦ Religious Society of Friends (Conservative)

Fundamentalist/Bible Churches
American Evangelical Christian Churches ♦ Baptist Bible Fellowship International ♦ Baptist Missionary Association of America ♦ Berean Fundamental Church ♦ Bible Fellowship Church ♦ Bible Presbyterian Church ♦ Christian and Missionary Alliance ♦ Christian Brethren (Plymouth Brethren) ♦ Conservative Baptist Association of America (CB America) ♦ Grace Gospel Fellowship ♦ Independent Fundamentalist Churches of America International Inc

Holiness Churches
Apostolic Christian Church of America ♦ Apostolic Faith Church ♦ Apostolic Overcoming Holy Church of God ♦ Church of Christ (Holiness) U.S.A ♦ Church of God (Holiness) ♦ Church of the Nazarene ♦ Churches of Christ in Christian Union ♦ Wesleyan Church

Hutterian Brethren

Islam
Nation of Islam ♦ Shi'ism ♦ Sufism ♦ Sunnism

Jehovah's Witness

Judaism
Conservative Judaism (United Synagogue of Conservative Judaism) ♦ Hasidic Judaism ♦ Orthodox Judaism (Orthodox Union) ♦ Reconstructionist Judaism (Jewish Reconstructionist Federation) ♦ Reform Judaism (Union of American Hebrew Congregations)

Latter-day Saints (Mormons)
Church of Christ (Temple Lot) ♦ Church of Jesus Christ (Bickertonites) ♦ Church of Jesus Christ of Latter-day Saints ♦ Reorganized Church of Jesus Christ of Latter-Day Saints

Lutheran Churches

Apostolic Lutheran Church of America ♦ Association of Free Lutheran Congregations ♦ Church of the Lutheran Brethren of America ♦ Church of the Lutheran Confession ♦ Evangelical Lutheran Church in America ♦ Evangelical Lutheran Synod ♦ Lutheran Church-Missouri Synod ♦ Wisconsin Evangelical Lutheran Synod

Mennonite Churches

Beachy Amish Mennonite Churches ♦ Bruderhof Communities ♦ Church of God in Christ, Mennonite ♦ Conservative Mennonite Conference ♦ Evangelical Mennonite Church ♦ Fellowship of Evangelical Bible Churches ♦ General Conference of Mennonite Brethren Churches ♦ Mennonite Church ♦ Missionary Church ♦ Old Order Amish Churches ♦ Old Order (Wisler) Mennonite Church

Methodist Churches

African Methodist Episcopal Church ♦ African Methodist Episcopal Zion Church ♦ Christian Methodist Episcopal Church ♦ Congregational Methodist Church ♦ Evangelical Church of North America ♦ Evangelical Congregational Church ♦ Evangelical Methodist Church ♦ Free Methodist Church of North America ♦ Pillar of Fire ♦ Primitive Methodist Church, U.S.A. ♦ Southern Methodist Church ♦ United Methodist Church ♦ Native American Religion

Orthodox and Oriental Orthodox Churches

African Orthodox Church ♦ Albanian Orthodox Archdiocese in America ♦ American Carpatho-Russian Orthodox Greek Catholic Church ♦ Antiochian Orthodox Christian Archdiocese of North America ♦ Armenian Church ♦ Bulgarian Eastern Orthodox Church ♦ Greek Orthodox Archdiocese of North America ♦ Holy Eastern Orthodox and Apostolic Church in North America, Inc ♦ Malankara Orthodox Syrian Church and Mar Thoma Orthodox Syrian Church (Indian Orthodox) ♦ Orthodox Church in America (Russian Orthodox) ♦ Romanian Orthodox Episcopate of America ♦ Serbian Eastern Orthodox Church ♦ Syrian Orthodox Church of Antioch (Archdiocese of the USA. & Canada) ♦ Ukrainian Orthodox Church of the U.S.A.

Pentecostal Churches

Assemblies of God, General Council of ♦ Assemblies of the Lord Jesus Christ ♦ Bible Way Church of our Lord Jesus Christ, World Wide, Inc. ♦ Christian Catholic Church ♦ Christian Church of North America, General Council ♦ Church of God (Cleveland, Tennessee) ♦ Church of God in Christ ♦ Church of God of Prophecy ♦ Church of Our Lord Jesus Christ of the Apostolic Faith, Inc. ♦ Church of the Living God, Christian Workers for Fellowship ♦ Church of the Living God, The Pillar and Ground of the Truth, Inc ♦ Congregational Holiness Church ♦ Elim Fellowship ♦ Full Gospel Fellowship of Churches and Ministers, International ♦ Independent Assemblies of God, International ♦ International Church of the Foursquare Gospel ♦ International Pentecostal Church of Christ ♦ International Pentecostal Holiness Church ♦ Open Bible Standard Churches, Inc. ♦ Pentecostal Assemblies of the World, Inc. ♦ Pentecostal Church of God ♦ Pentecostal Free Will Baptist Church, Inc. ♦ United Holy Church of America, Inc. ♦ United Pentecostal Church International ♦ Vineyard Churches International

Presbyterian Churches

Associate Reformed Presbyterian Church ♦ Cumberland Presbyterian Church ♦ Cumberland Presbyterian Church in America ♦ Evangelical Presbyterian Church ♦ Korean-American Presbyterian Church ♦ Orthodox Presbyterian Church ♦ Presbyterian Church in America ♦ Presbyterian Church (U.S.A.) ♦ Reformed Presbyterian Church of North America

Reformed Churches

Christian Reformed Church in North America ♦ Hungarian Reformed Church in America ♦ Netherlands Reformed Congregations in North America ♦ Protestant Reformed Churches in America ♦ Reformed Church in America ♦ Reformed Church in the United States

Salvation Army (and related organizations)

American Rescue Workers ♦ Salvation Army ♦ Volunteers of America, Inc.

Schwenkfelder Church

Spiritualist and Theosophical Bodies

National Spiritual Alliance of the U.S.A ♦ National Spiritualist Association of Churches ♦ Swedenborgian Church (The General Convention of the New Jerusalem in the U.S.A.)

Triumph the Church and Kingdom of God in Christ, International

Unification Church

Unitarian Universalist Association

Unity School of Christianity and Association of Unity Churches

Universal Fellowship of Metropolitan Community Churches

Worldwide Church of God

——— ♦ ———

Appendix B

This Appendix B definitions are derived and summarized from *Sparkling Gems from the Greek (Volume I)*. Copyright© 2003 by Rick Renner. Used by permission of Rick Renner. For an in-depth detailed discussion of each act, you are encouraged to study *Pages 492-517*.

———◆———

GALATIANS 5:19
Acts of a Flesh Nature

NKJV: Gal 5:19-21. Now the works of the *flesh[4561]* are evident, which are: *adultery[9999]*, *fornication[4202]*, *uncleanness[0167]*, *lewdness[0766]*, *idolatry[1495]*, *sorcery[5331]*, *hatred[2189]*, *contentions[2054]*, *jealousies[2205]*, *outbursts of wrath[2372]*, *selfish ambitions[2052]*, *dissensions[1370]*, *heresies[0139]*, *envy[5355]*, *murders[9999]*, *drunkenness[3178]*, *revelries[2970]*, *and the like*; of which I tell you beforehand, just as I also told you in time past, that **those who practice such things will not inherit the kingdom of God.**

[9999] Inserted word; <u>not</u> in the original Greek manuscripts.

NKJV: Gal 6:7-8. Do not be deceived, God is not mocked; for whatever a man sows, that he will also reap. For he who sows to his **flesh** will of the flesh reap corruption, but he who sows to the **Spirit** will of the Spirit reap everlasting life.

This **Appendix B** contains a detailed description of each act of a **sinful flesh nature**. The Greek to English translations are quite misleading in many instances. In many instances, the underlying Greek word will shock and surprise the often malformed perception inferred by its English translation counterpart.

- *NKJV = New King James Version.*
- *KJV = King James Version*
- *Greek = Underlying Greek Word*
- *NSECB = Short definitions from the New Strong's Exhaustive Concordance.*

The NKJV version word translations are used in this Appendix B. Other versions often contain very diverse translation word choices. Therefore, it is very important that we understand the *true meaning and full implication* of each underlying *Greek* word.

4561flesh[NKJV&KJV], **sarx***[Greek]*. *Flesh (as stripped of the skin), i.e. (strictly) the meat of an animal (as food), or (by extension) the body (as opposed to the soul [or spirit], or as the symbol of what is external, or as the means of kindred), or (by implication) human nature (with its frailties [physically or morally] and passions), or (specifically) a human being (as such).*[NSECB] This word is used to depict sinful impulses and carnal cravings. I must control the flesh otherwise the flesh will go to work and manifest these ultimately fatal impulses and cravings. This is the "inherited flesh nature" that I focused on in the previous segments.

9999adultery[NKJV&KJV] Inserted word; not in the original Greek manuscripts.

4202fornication[NKJV&KJV] **porneia***[Greek]*. *Harlotry (including adultery and incest); figuratively, idolatry* [NSECB]. This Greek word includes all sexual activity outside of a heterosexual marriage, homosexuality, prostitution and anyone who has sexual relations with a prostitute.

0167uncleanness[NKJV&KJV] **akatharsia***[Greek]*. *Impurity (the quality), physically or morally* [NSECB]. This Greek word refers to lewd or unclean thoughts that can eventually produce lewd or unclean actions. This word suggests that actions begin in the mind as unclean thoughts before they manifest as unclean deeds – I must allow the Holy Spirit to guide my minds and thoughts.

0766lewdness[NKJV] **lasciviousness***[KJV]* **aselgeia***[Greek]*. *From a compound of 1 (as a negative particle) and a presumed selges; licentiousness (sometimes including other vices)* [NSECB]. This Greek word refers to the excessive consumption of food or wild, undisciplined living that is especially marked by unbridled sex. This means that in God's mind, it is just as perverted to overindulge in food as it is to engage in sinful sexual activities! The word aselgeia is listed as a principal sin of the cities of Sodom and Gomorrah (see 2Peter 2:7) and the reason that God overthrew them.

1495idolatry[NKJV&KJV] **eidololatria***[Greek]*. *Image-worship (literally or figuratively)* [NSECB]. This Greek word refers to the worship of idols. Idolatry exists anytime I give complete and undivided attention, devotion, passion, love or commitment to a person or object other than God. Idols can sneak into our lives. If I'm not careful, my focus can turn away from God to the degree that I worship spouse, children, parents, job, vision, possessions, school, and even church activities – God is not willing to share His Lordship in my life with anything or anyone.

5331sorcery[NKJV] **witchcraft***[KJV]* **pharmakeia***[Greek]*. *Medication ("pharmacy"), i.e. (by extension) magic (literally or figuratively)* [NSECB]. This Greek word refers to medicines or drugs that are mind altering. Pagan religions used drugs to alter the state of a person's mind. Pagan worshipers frequented pagan temples for relief from sickness and problems – the pagan priests mixed drugs into wine vials and gave it to the worshipers to drink. The only way these worships experienced relief from their problems was to return again and again for more doses of drugs. Our flesh behaves the same as the pagan priests in that it doesn't know how to fix itself and doesn't want to be fixed. Our flesh hates confrontation. If I refuse to truly look at my true self I can blindly develop chemical dependencies to avoid seeing the truth.

2189hatred^NKJV&KJV echthra^Greek. Feminine of 2190; hostility; by implication, a reason for opposition ^NSECB. This Greek word expresses the idea of intense hostility that I can feel toward someone else – someone I just cannot seem to get along with. If I let the flesh control, I will hold onto the grudge. I must reject the flesh control, seek reconciliation and walk in the Holy Spirit – replace the hostility and animosity with love and peace.

2054contentions^NKJV variance^KJV eris^Greek. Of uncertain affinity; a quarrel, i.e. (by implication) wrangling ^NSECB. This Greek word depicts a bitter spirit that is consumed with its own self-interests and self-ambitions – a spirit that would rather split and divide than admit it is wrong. This spirit causes churches to split and families to dissolve. Our flesh hates to surrender or to admit it is wrong or to let someone else be right. I must reject my flesh's desire to seek its own self-interests at all cost and replace any bitter wrangling spirit with the guidance of a loving Holy Spirit.

2205jealousies^NKJV emulations^KJV zelos^Greek. Properly, heat, i.e. (figuratively) "zeal" (in a favorable sense, ardor; in an unfavorable one, jealousy, as of a husband [figuratively, of God], or an enemy, malice) ^NSECB. This Greek word depicts the fervor of someone who is passionately upset because someone else achieved more or received more. The story of Joseph's brothers in Egypt is an example, where Acts 7:9 uses the word "zeloo". Jealousy is such a strong force that it can move us into regrettable actions when it starts to operate. Jealousy is a work of the flesh that brings great hurt and destruction. I must guard against such envy or jealousy – seeking the guidance of the Holy Spirit and instead rejoicing with others.

2372wrath^NKJV&KJV thumos^Greek. Passion (as if breathing hard) ^NSECB. This Greek word describes us when we are literally boiling with anger about something. Rather than take a perceived offense to the Cross, I choose to meditate on the offense. The longer I think about it, the more upset I become until one day something happens that triggers a release of our rage – that is the way our flesh tries to deal with a problem. Confronting people and problems is challenging but it is the mature loving path – on the other hand, the route of our flesh is to delay issues and erupt in madness. I must crucify my flesh desire in its place and deal with my situation when it first happens – seeking the guidance of the Holy Spirit to resolve my perceived offense.

2052selfish ambitions^NKJV strife^KJV eritheia^Greek. Properly, intrigue, i.e. (by implication)^NSECB. This Greek word describes a person who is selfishly concerned about his own wants, desires and pleasures without considering the same needs in others – a person so self-consumed that he becomes blinded to the needs and ambitions of others. It is the nature of our carnal flesh to be self-consumed, however, when I have this attitude, I am bound to hurt and offend people. I must think of how I can be a blessing to others rather than being focused on how others can bless me. God's Spirit resides inside each of us from the very moment of conception. Abortion advocates would do well to think through this enlightenment. I must yield to the guidance of the Holy Spirit and be compassionate and caring about the needs of others.

*1370*dissensions*NKJV* seditions*KJV* dichostsis*Greek*. *Disunion, i.e. (figuratively) dissension* *NSECB*. This Greek word describes a person who rebels and steps away from someone to whom he should have been loyal. Our flesh hates rules and regulations imposed upon it. Children rebel against parents, wives rebel against their husbands, churches rebel against pastors, and people rebel against God. Our world's conflicts are usually due to a flesh that defies authority and rules it doesn't want to accept! This is the reason a little baby throws food across the room – the reason this young child can act so defiantly is that he is wrapped in flesh – and one of the works of the flesh is to be rebellious and defiant! I must not give into my carnal desires and not abandon my God-appointed leaders. My loyalty is important – my disloyalty is hurtful and destructive. Give to Caesar what is Caesar's and to God what is God's *Matt 12:17*. I must stand by those whom God has called to be my leaders.

*0139*heresies*NKJV&KJV* hairesis*Greek*. *Properly, a choice, i.e. (specially) a party or (abstractly) disunion* *NSECB*. This Greek word carries the idea of a person or group of people who are sectarian. In New Testament times, these groups were considered to be unauthorized because they were not submitted to the authority of the church leadership. If allowed to do so, our flesh will separate us into a faction and gravitate to others who also want to believe they are better than others. If we let all that flesh gather in one place, an elite clique inside the church will form such that no one else will be able to get in. I must always realize that we are all part of the whole Body of Christ. God has not given any of us a revelation of truth so special that it places us in a higher spiritual class. I must override my flesh carnality and come down to reality – I must get busy loving and serving all brothers and sisters in a local church.

*5355*envy*NKJV* envyings*KJV* phthonos*Greek*. *Ill-will (as detraction), i.e. jealousy (spite)* *NSECB*. This Greek word implies a deeply felt grudge because someone possesses what a person wishes was his own. It is when I begrudge what another person possesses and I covet that person's belongings, accomplishments, relationships, or titles in life. The word describes us when I friend someone when in truth all I want is their job or position. This kind of behavior is hurtful, manipulative, and unkind. The chief priests were envious of the acclaim Jesus was gaining, so to get rid of the competition, the chief priests decided to kill Jesus. This type of envy is so strong that it propels us to take some kind of action designed to do away with the person who has the advantage. When I find myself tempted to get envious over someone else's blessing or position, I must call upon the Spirit of God to help me mortify that deed of the flesh. I must let the Holy Spirit guide me into rejoicing when someone else gets blessed! What I sow is exactly what I will reap.

*3178***drunkenness**^{NKJV&KJV} **methe**^{Greek}. *An intoxicant, i.e. (by implication) intoxication* ^{NSECB}. This Greek word refers to strong drink or to drunkenness. The consumption of wine for the sake of intoxication was common in the first century due to many pagan religions that employed wine as a part of their religious practices. An intoxicated state suppresses our mind's ability to think correctly and then releases our flesh to fully express itself – sometimes not so good. Since I am to walk free from the power of my flesh, the last thing I need is to drink wine to intoxication and then do things that are of a flesh nature and damaging. I must avoid the undisciplined consumption of wine that leads to the works of the carnal flesh.

*2970***revelries**^{NKJV} **revellings**^{KJV} **komos**^{Greek}. *A carousal (as if letting loose)* ^{NSECB}. This Greek word describes a festive procession or merry-making (some versions translate "orgies" which is very misleading). This word describes a person who can't bear the thought of boredom. This person lives for the next fun, next meal, next movie, next vacation, next etc. Our flesh wants to escape responsibility, thrive on fun, and avoid the seriousness of life. If we let our flesh lead us, we will waste our time and energies on things that are not eternal – with nothing to show for it but maybe lots of credit card debt. The truth is there is plenty to do. I could be reading my bible; playing with my children; developing my relationship with my brothers and sisters; visiting my neighbors; volunteering to serve in some area of my church; mowing my yard; learning to cook; cleaning my garage; or reading a book and developing my mind. Reasonable fun, entertainment and vacations are necessary and healthy for each of us – on the other hand, excess striving to escape boredom, maturity and responsibility is a devastating work of the carnal flesh. It is imperative that I seek the guidance of the Holy Spirit.

———— ♦ ————

Appendix C

Page Index to Scripture Verses

Appendix C

Page Index to Scripture Verses

———— ◆ ————